EAST OF IRELAI
– ON RIVER AND CANAL
A WALKING GUIDE

LENNY ANTONELLI is a journalist and writer whose focus is the outdoors and the environment. He contributes to a variety of national and international publications. A keen walker and camper, he is happiest when outside.

Stay up to date with the author at www.lennyantonelli.ie and twitter.com/lennyantonelli

Shra Bridge on the Grand Canal

Disclaimer

Hillwalking, mountaineering and walking are risk sports. The author and The Collins Press accept no responsibility for any injury, loss or inconvenience sustained by anyone using this guidebook.

Acknowledgements

Every townland in Ireland seems to have at least one person who could tell you a story about each hedgerow and field. I am indebted to all the local experts who reviewed drafts of particular walks and willingly offered local stories and history. My thanks to Michael Bane, Jenny Blackford, Geoff Clarke, Sean Conroy, Eamonn Doran, Hugh Fanning, Ann Lannigan, James Leahy, Ben McCabe, Coilin MacLochlainn, John McKeown, Donal Magner, Christopher Moriarty, John Mullen, Jimmy Murphy and Rosanna Nolan. I am grateful also to Katrina McGirr at Waterways Ireland for all her help. Thanks to Una McMahon for taking some of the photos, and to Ciaran Cuddy, Elias Spinn and Audrey Reilly for contributing images too. And thanks to Ruth McNally for her diligent proofreading and support.

Spin Bridge on the Royal Canal

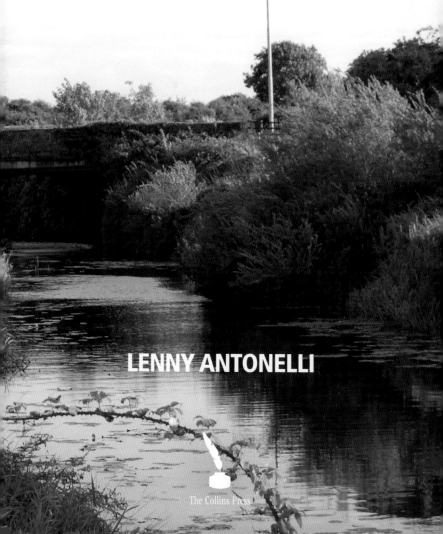

EAST OF IRELAND WALKS
– ON RIVER AND CANAL
A WALKING GUIDE

LENNY ANTONELLI

The Collins Press

F<small>IRST PUBLISHED IN</small> 2015 <small>BY</small>
The Collins Press
West Link Park
Doughcloyne
Wilton
Cork

A CIP record for this book is available from the British Library.

Paperback ISBN: 978-1-84889-238-5

Design and typesetting by Fairways Design

Typeset in Myriad Pro

Printed in Poland by Białostockie Zakłady Graficzne SA

Oak tree by the River Nore

Contents

The Nore

The Barrow Way

The Derry River

The Avonmore

The Vartry

Select Bibliography

Towpath along the Royal Canal

Route Location Map

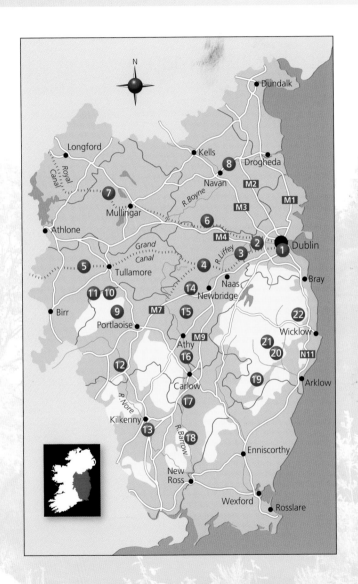

Quick-Reference Route Table

No.	Route
The Dodder	
1	Ringsend to Firhouse (Dublin city)
The Liffey	
2	Lucan to Leixlip (Counties Dublin & Kildare)
The Grand Canal	
3 (a)	Lucan Road Bridge to Hazelhatch (Counties Dublin & Kildare)
3 (b)	Hazelhatch to Sallins (County Kildare)
4 (a)	Milltown Feeder: Milltown to Lowtown (County Kildare)
4 (b)	Pollardstown Fen (County Kildare)
5 (a)	Tullamore to Pollagh (County Offaly)
5 (b)	Pollagh to Ferbane (County Offaly)
The Royal Canal	
6	Enfield to Kilcock (Counties Meath & Kildare)
7 (a)	Mullingar to Coolnahay (County Westmeath)
7 (b)	Coolnahay to Ballynacargy (County Westmeath)
The Boyne	
8	Boyne Ramparts Walk, Navan to Stackallen (County Meath)
The Barrow	
9	Old Mill Loop, Glenbarrow (County Laois)
The Clodiagh	
10	Brittas Loop, Clonaslee (County Laois)
The Silver River	
11 (a)	Paul's Lane Loop (County Offaly)
11 (b)	Silver River (Counties Offaly & Laois)
The Nore	
12	Dunmore Woods Loop, Durrow (County Laois)
13	Nore Valley Way, Kilkenny to Bennettsbridge (County Kilkenny)
The Barrow Way	
14 (a)	Robertstown to Rathangan (County Kildare)
14 (b)	Rathangan to Monasterevin (County Kildare)
15 (a)	Monasterevin to Vicarstown (Counties Kildare & Laois)
15 (b)	Vicarstown to Athy (Counties Laois & Kildare)
16 (a)	Athy to Maganey (County Kildare)
16 (b)	Maganey to Carlow (Counties Kildare & Carlow)
17 (a)	Carlow to Leighlinbridge (Counties Carlow & Laois)
17 (b)	Leighlinbridge to Goresbridge (County Carlow)
18 (a)	Goresbridge to Graiguenamanagh (County Carlow)
18 (b)	Graiguenamanagh to St Mullin's (County Carlow)
The Derry River	
19	Railway Walk & Tomnafinnoge Wood River Walk (County Wicklow)
The Avonmore	
20	River Walk, Avondale Forest Park (County Wicklow)
21	Blue Loop, Vale of Clara Nature Reserve (County Wicklow)
The Vartry	
22	Waterfall Walk, The Devil's Glen (County Wicklow)

Category	Grade	Distance	Time	Page
River	Moderate	14km	3½–4½ hours	
River	Easy	6km	1½–2 hours	
Canal	Easy	4.5km	1–1½ hours	
Canal	Moderate	12.5km	3–4 hours	
Canal	Moderate	8km	2–2½ hours	
Canal	Easy	4km	1–1½ hours	
Canal	Moderate	15.5km	4–5 hours	
Canal	Moderate	12.5km	3–4 hours	
Canal	Moderate	13km	3–4 hours	
Canal	Moderate	10.5km	2½–3½ hours	
Canal	Moderate	8km	2–3 hours	
River	Easy	6.5km	1½–2½ hours	
River	Strenuous	10km	3–4 hours	
River	Moderate	6.5km	2–2½ hours	
River	Moderate	5km	2–2½ hours	
River	Moderate	12km	3–4 hours	
River	Moderate	15km	3½–5 hours	
River	Moderate	13km	3–4 hours	
Canal	Moderate	14km	3½–4½ hours	
Canal	Moderate	10.5km	2½–3½ hours	
Canal	Moderate	12km	3–4 hours	
Canal	Moderate	10.5km	2½–3½ hours	
River & canal	Moderate	10.5km	2½–3½ hours	
River & canal	Easy	8.5km	2–3 hours	
River & canal	Moderate	11km	2½–3½ hours	
River & canal	Moderate	14.5km	3½–5 hours	
River & canal	Moderate	14.5 km	3½–5 hours	
River & canal	Easy	8km	2–2½ hours	
River	Easy	10km	2½–3½ hours	
River	Moderate	5km	2–2½ hours	
River	Moderate	9.5km	2½–3½ hours	
River	Moderate	5km	2–2½ hours	

Waterfall on the Glenbarrow
gorge (Route 9)

Introduction

Canals and rivers seem similar, but are really quite different. Canals are wrought from human engineering and labour, but have become colonised by nature: by reeds, rushes, willows, weeds, pike, perch and more. They are more sedate and less wild than rivers, being composed of straight lines, right angles and still water. Stepping onto a canal towpath to take a walk is liberating. When you do, you enter the private world of canals, which stretches unbroken for long distances across Ireland, changing only subtly along the way. This world bears little relation to the one outside it, and it has a forgotten architecture all of its own: locks, bridges, aqueducts, quays, towpaths and lock houses.

Rivers, on the other hand, are wild: they are carved by nature. Though they may have have been dammed, dredged and re-routed, they retain their original spirit. Rivers widen and contract, bend and curve. They lack straight lines and right angles. The American essayist Barry Lopez wrote that a river can't be known: 'If it's a man's intent to spend thirty years staring at a river's environs in order to arrive at an explanation of the river, he should find some other way to spend his time,' he wrote. 'The reason this is true is because the river is not a thing,' but rather '... an expression of biological life, in dynamic relation to everything around it'.

This book will introduce you to walks by rivers and canals in the east and midlands of Ireland. These range from short loops to a five-day trek. This is not an exhaustive selection of river and canal walks, just a good sample.

These walks are, by their nature, mostly flat, relatively straight and easy to navigate. Most are on existing trails, and while giving basic directions, I focus on each waterway's history, wildlife and folklore too. I also hope to capture something of the quality of each place – from its light and water to its flora and fauna – during the time I spent there researching this book. I am sure your experience of each walk will be different but equally as singular.

Happy trails

Lenny Antonelli

Some advice on these walks

All rivers can flood during and after rainfall. They often rise quickly and can flood nearby trails. I would advise checking on local conditions before embarking, particularly during rainy periods and in the wetter months.

Most of these walks are on relatively flat, easy terrain. Some, such as those in Slieve Blooms or the Wicklow valleys, involve ascending and descending rougher trails. When I started this book, I intended to specify which walks had wet and muddy ground but soon realised this applies to pretty much all of them, even parts of the more urban walks, so wear good waterproof footwear.

I have based my walking times on a speed of 3 to 4km per hour, which is a slow-to-moderate pace, but fairly normal for me on flat terrain when I am enjoying the scenery and taking short breaks along the way. Leave more time if taking longer breaks. I have rounded distances to the nearest kilometre or half kilometre, and times to the nearest hour or half hour.

Some of these walks make long, tiring days out, at over 20km, and I have tried to show how these might be broken down in subsections if desired.

Many of the walks are linear and I have described them in the direction I walked them, which was normally based on the convenience of transport. I have used the terms 'left' and 'right' bank of the river or canal, relative to the direction I walked, rather than east or west, etc., as this is a more practical description for the walker in the field.

Unlike mountain walks, which cross open upland terrain, river and canal walks follow fairly strict linear routes along waterways. Most of these walks are on existing trails or paths, and maps for many can be downloaded online. Most are well marked, meaning a map may not be essential. But I still find it useful to bring one, particularly on longer walks, if only to track my progress and look for landmarks.

It may seem obvious, but take care at road crossings. On the canals, road bridges are humped to allow boats to pass under. This makes it very difficult to see traffic coming over the bridge. These bridges are sometimes near blind corners too, and usually have no footpath. So take your time and pay attention.

Where a trail has been graded (easy, moderate, strenuous, etc.), I have given that grading. These grades tend to be quite relative to one's experience. For example, a trail graded strenuous would not trouble an experienced hillwalker much. Where no grading was available, I have offered my own description of the trail's suitability.

In some instances, the official length given for a walk on the map board at the trailhead differs from GPS measurements. In this book, I have used the GPS measurements.

Be aware of Lyme disease, which some ticks carry. To protect myself I wear full-length trousers (and tuck them into my socks when in long grass) and check myself for ticks during and after walks. Insect repellent can deter ticks too. It is also a good idea to have a tick remover, which can be bought cheaply. For more information see www.ticktalkireland.org and www.lymediseaseaction.org.uk.

Responsible wild camping is allowed on the towpaths of navigations controlled by Waterways Ireland (i.e. the Grand Canal, Royal Canal and Barrow). Familiarise yourself with the Leave No Trace code (www.lnt.org), and do not light fires. Elsewhere, you would need to ask permission before camping on private land. This particularly applies to farmland and land near houses and buildings. In remote forests and woodlands, I have never encountered problems wild camping if I pitch my tent late and leave early, camp away from trails, and leave no trace.

Waterways Ireland sometimes closes stretches of its navigations for maintenance, particularly outside summer. Check the Marine Notices section of www.waterwaysireland.org before embarking. At the time of writing this was under the News section of the website.

Do not bring dogs on trails where livestock may be encountered.

Finally, please note that the layout of marked trails is sometimes altered for various reasons. If the waymarkers you encounter differ from directions in this book, conditions on the ground should take precedence.

THE DODDER

Ringsend to Firhouse
(Dublin city)

[handwritten notes:] May 19
Ringsend to Millmount weir
+ return
Fannes Brown's cafe

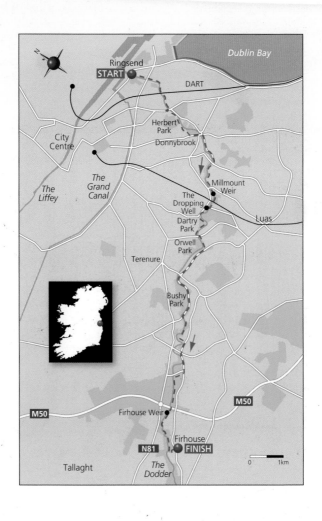

The Dodder at Ringsend, with the Aviva Stadium on the right (courtesy Una McMahon)

Overview: Flat walk along the River Dodder through the parklands and suburbs of south Dublin city.

Trail: No specific trail: you are following paths by the river through connecting suburban parks. Use pedestrian crossings on roads.

Suitability: Flat walking on footpaths that are almost always bike, wheelchair and buggy friendly. The full route makes a long walk but it can easily be broken up into smaller chunks.

Start: Ringsend Bridge on Bridge Street, the main street through Ringsend village in Dublin 4, right beside St Patrick's Church. Ringsend is well serviced by Dublin Bus.

Finish: Dodder Valley Park, Firhouse Road West, Dublin 24. Bus stop number 3004 on Ballycullen Avenue, which is just across the road from the park, is serviced by Dublin Bus to the city centre.

Distance & time: 14km, 3½ to 4½ hours.
The walk passes through Ballsbridge, Donnybrook, Clonskeagh, Milltown, Dartry and Rathfarnham so could easily be broken into stages accessed by Dublin Bus. The Green Line of the Luas also serves Milltown.

Alternative routes: Another great walk on the Dodder is to follow the Dublin Mountains Way from Sean Walsh Park in Tallaght to the Bohernabreena Reservoir in the Glenasmole valley, a walk of about 10km one-way.

Map & further info: Bring any good street map of Dublin or use good digital mapping to find your way.

Looking down the Dodder near Milltown

The art of urban walking was perfected by the flâneurs, the fashionable idlers of nineteenth-century Paris. For a while some even walked tortoises on leashes, to ensure a slow and thoughtful exploration of the city. I'm not suggesting you bring a tortoise with you, but like all walks, the Dodder rewards those who pay closest attention. Today, Dublin revolves around its roads. But walking the Dodder introduces you to an older thoroughfare, towards which the city once turned.

Start from Ringsend Bridge, where the tidal Dodder is tightly held between stone walls. Before the eighteenth century most of this area was tidal, and the settlements of Ringsend and Irishtown were on raised sandbanks, isolated from the mainland. Even after the river was tamed, Ringsend was a refuge for outlaws, infamous for burglaries and highway robberies. It also became a popular seaside resort in the eighteenth century.

Follow the left bank of the Dodder south along Fitzwilliam Quay. Far ahead you can see the Dublin Mountains, where this river rises.

This is a fine spot for casual birdwatching. Walking here in spring, I watched a little egret foraging in the shallows. These small, white herons began breeding in Ireland only in 1997, but are now common on our coasts. Their breeding plumage is extravagant, and was once in such demand for hat-making that it nearly drove the species to extinction. Gulls and cormorants are common here too.

The pump house on the left just before Londonbridge Road was built in 1881 to pump sewage to the Ringsend wastewater treatment plant. Cross the road and follow the left bank of the Dodder as you approach the Aviva Stadium. Look for the plaque on the wall opposite where the Swan River enters the Dodder, which quotes from James Joyce's novel *Finnegans Wake*: 'Shake hands through the thicketloch! Sweet swanwater!'

There has been much work along the Lower Dodder recently to improve the footpaths and prevent flooding. In spring, grey mullet come here from the sea to shoal. This fish is notoriously hard to catch, because it feeds mainly on plankton rather than larger organisms.

The path emerges onto Herbert Road, where I have sometimes seen foxes at night. Cross the road and continue by the river under the railway and into Ballsbridge. You can join the right bank of the river across the road by the Herbert Park Hotel. The weir just before the hotel marks the highest point the tide reaches on the Dodder.

Up ahead, steps bring you down to a quiet and shaded stretch of water. Down here at the river's level, the foliage hides you from the city. When I first walked the Dodder here, the trees were strewn with weathered rubbish, like bunting. When the river floods, rubbish fly-tipped upstream is deposited further down. Every year, however, the Dodder Action Group undertakes a huge clean-up to restore the river.

The path leaves the river and heads into Herbert Park, where you turn left (if you didn't take the steps down to the water, keep straight). In 1907 a World's Fair was held here. The organisers constructed a vast central palace with four wings, along with other buildings. Now, however, only the bandstand and pond remain.

When you reach a residential street, go left and follow Eglinton Terrace out to Donnybrook. You can rejoin the river across the main road a few hundred metres to your left, following the footpath along Beaver Row. Until 1741 there was no bridge here, only a ford. The old houses of Beaver Row were built for workers from the mills and quarries that once thrived nearby.

For over 600 years, this stretch of the Dodder hosted the revelry of the Donnybrook Fair. But this ancient festival proved too debauched for the authorities, and it was banned during the nineteenth century. The author Elrington Ball made it sound like tremendous fun, describing it as 'an occasion of drunkenness, riot and moral degradation which were a disgrace to Ireland'.

The first waterfall along Beaver Row marks the highest point to which most salmon and sea trout come up the Dodder. The second waterfall, under the derelict Smurfit paper mill, is enclosed within a weir. Beaver Row then becomes Beech Hill Road and emerges at Clonskeagh. Cross the road and follow the path through parkland on the left bank of the river as it becomes more wooded.

Cross Dundrum Road when you reach it, and keep on the left bank of the river. Soon Millmount weir appears. The remains of an old millrace are nearby.

The river takes a sharp turn right, and the nine arches of Milltown Viaduct appear. Today this elegant structure supports the Green Line of the Luas, but it was originally built in 1846 for the railway that served Milltown, Dundrum, Stillorgan, Foxrock, and Bray from Harcourt Street.

The path joins Patrick Doyle Road then emerges by Classon's Bridge. Turn right to cross the bridge to reach the Dropping Well pub, which dates from

Millmount weir

Famine times, when it was also a morgue. Go through the car park behind it to reach the river, where there is a bronze statue of a rhinoceros on the water. Nobody ever claimed responsibility after it mysteriously appeared overnight in 2002.

On the Dodder near Rathfarnham (courtesy Ciaran Cuddy)

The path then leaves the river and joins Milltown Road. Turn left, and then, a bit further on, left again by the old Dartry Dye Works building, and go down a quiet lane into Dartry Park. Here the river meanders in wide arcs and, when the water is low, its sandy banks are exposed. Low weirs provide pools for brown trout here. You pass a larger weir, then come to the tunnel under Orwell Road. Climb up to the road and cross the bridge to rejoin the river on its left bank. The land across the river here – now Orwell Park – was once owned by the Bewley family, whose cattle grazed it and provided milk for the Bewley cafés.

In his book *Down the Dodder*, the naturalist Christopher Moriarty writes that when the park opened, it had a paddling pool with a concrete submarine. 'It was the place where, at about the age of ten, I made my first encounter with an eel,' he writes. Moriarty carried the exhausted eel, which had been trying to escape the pool, back to the river. This part of the river is still home to eels, which must make their way up all the weirs and falls from Ringsend.

Ahead on the left is the old gate of Rathfarnham Castle. Built in the 1770s, it served as a lived-in gatehouse until the 1940s. Kingfishers inhabit this stretch of the river. I've also been surprised to look up here and see herons, the most Zen-like of birds, standing motionless high in the trees. Watch out for mandarin ducks too, a brilliant ornamental species.

Just past the gate there is a low path along the left bank of the river. Soon you come to Rathfarnham weir. The millrace on the opposite bank is overgrown, and sparrowhawks have been known to nest there in the foliage. The path emerges onto Lower Dodder Road.

Follow the footpath and go right at the fork past some houses to Rathfarnham Road. The single-arch bridge to your right was built in 1765. During the Second World War holes were drilled in it to hold explosives in case of invasion.

Cross the road and follow the path back down to the river's left bank. In parts there is a riverside path, while in others you follow the footpath by the road. But further ahead you can cross a footbridge into Bushy Park, which developed beside a nineteenth-century Georgian manor. You can follow either side of the river from there. Bushy Park has ornamental ponds, lawns and exotic trees. Nearby, the Owendoher River, flowing from the Dublin Mountains, joins the Dodder. This stream was once important for restoring water levels in the river, which had been left dry by mills upstream. A local man told me it was a good place to see dippers and foxes too. There was also once a limestone quarry here.

The paths on both sides of the river go under Springfield Avenue. Beyond here, you need to continue on the left bank, so if you are on the right, climb up and cross the bridge. Follow the path into a small park. Where the path splits in two a second time, go left away from the river into Kilvere housing estate. Turn left to reach Butterfield Avenue, then go right and straight on through the junction. You can rejoin the river half a kilometre down the road by entering Dodder Valley Park, on your right just after another junction, and following the path straight down to the riverbank, where you go left.

This is the best stretch of the urban Dodder, perhaps because it is the least urban, flowing through scrub, grassland and woods. I once watched a huge murmuration of starlings swoop and dive here across the dim winter sky.

Following the river, you pass under the M50 and emerge at the mighty Firhouse weir, built from giant limestone blocks. It dates from the thirteenth century, when it was built to raise the level of the Dodder to carry its water by channel to the River Poddle, 2km north.

Firhouse weir (courtesy Ciaran Cuddy)

From there these rivers delivered water to a basin on James's Street, now in Dublin 8, providing water for the growing city of Dublin. The Dodder and Poddle provided most of the city's water until the eighteenth century.

Further on, the Dodder spreads its fingers around small scrubby islands. Christopher Moriarty calls this 'the island wilderness,' and it is perhaps the only untouched part of the urban Dodder. Damp-loving willow and alder thrive here, and this micro-wilderness is rich in wildflowers too. Ponds on the islets provide a habitat for frogs and newts, and there is also abundant birdlife here.

Follow the course of the river as the path curves to the left and emerges at the entrance of the park on Firhouse Road, back in modern Dublin.

THE LIFFEY ✓ Country Park. Jan 19.

Lucan to Leixlip
(Counties Dublin & Kildare)

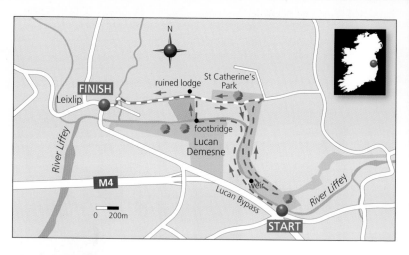

Grassland at St Catherine's Park (courtesy Una McMahon)

Overview: Scenic stroll by the Liffey through parklands and ancient woods.

Trail: No specific marked trail, just park and woodland paths.

Suitability: Easy, mostly flat walk on well-paved paths. Would also be accessible by bike, buggy or wheelchair, except for the upper section in St Catherine's Wood.

Start: Lucan Demesne car park is on the R835 Lucan-to-Leixlip road about 800m from Lucan Main Street (facing the Garda station, turn right). Lucan is well serviced by Dublin Bus.

Finish: Mill Lane, just off Main Street, Leixlip. Alternatively, return to your start point. Leixlip is serviced by Dublin Bus; Leixlip Confey train station has regular services to and from Connolly Station.

Distance & time: 6km, 1½ to 2 hours.

Alternative routes: You can also walk along the Liffey at the Irish National War Memorial Gardens, Islandbridge and at Waterstown Park in Palmerstown.

Map & further info: The area is covered by OSi *Discovery Series* Sheet 50, but no map is essential really. Or use any good digital maps.

The Liffey that most people see is not the real Liffey. Through Dublin city it is a poor excuse for a river, a dull soup edging towards the sea. But between Lucan and Leixlip the suburbs fade to fields, and here you can find the real river, which is youthful, quick and clear.

Go through the gate at the top of the Lucan Demesne car park and follow the path down to the water. This was once the site of Lucan Spa, a natural sulphur well. The spa was said to smell of rotten eggs at its strongest, but drinking the mineral-rich water was said to be therapeutic, and bottles were once sold from a hut here.

Follow the path as the river widens into a delta of channels and islands, under an old weir. I last walked here in March, just as spring arrived. The daffodils were out fresh, and from the bank I watched an early-season angler cast into the water.

At the fork, go right to stay with the river. Here the path is lined with oaks; some are recently planted, but others are old and gnarly, dating from the

The author under an oak by the Liffey (courtesy Una McMahon)

Wood anemones by the Liffey (courtesy Una McMahon)

eighteenth century. Keep an eye out for grey squirrels – I watched one dart across the thinnest of branches from one tree to the next. Look out for otters and kingfishers on the river too.

Stay with the riverside path until you reach the footbridge, then cross it, following the sign for St Catherine's Park. You might notice an odd sweet smell: Leixlip's wastewater treatment plant is ahead on your left.

The history of Lucan demesne and St Catherine's goes back to the twelfth century, when King Henry II seized these lands from the Irish. He granted them to the Lord of Lucan, Warris de Peche, who in turn offered them to the Order of St Victor, which founded the Priory of St Catherine. At the time it was fashionable for Anglo-Norman lords to establish religious foundations to save their souls, and those of their ancestors.

After crossing the footbridge, follow the path to the ruined lodge of Lucan Demesne. The architect Francis Johnston is believed to have designed it for the La Touche family, along with a three-storey manor, around 1790. But a fire destroyed the big house within a decade, and it was never rebuilt.

Trinity College pharmacy professor Christopher O'Connor owned this land in the 1940s and 1950s, and grew exotic plants such as deadly nightshade, peppermint, carnations and poppies, which he sent to a pharmaceutical plant in Tipperary for processing. The Office of Public Works bought the estate in 1996.

Turn right by the ruined lodge to follow the 'Woodland Walk' sign. Highland cattle and Jacob sheep were introduced to the grasslands here to improve the diversity of plant life. The animals graze and trample some parts of the field more than others, creating a richer habitat. You pass a ruined church, once a private chapel for the estate, which dates from the eighteenth century. Further down on the left is a dark stand of spruce and fir, and beside the path is a monstrous old beech tree.

When you come to the bench, turn right. Leaving the field behind, you enter what might be the oldest wood in Dublin.

I am somewhat obsessed with old woods. I have spent long hours staring at maps and poring over botanical research to learn about Ireland's ancient woodlands. In the same way some people are driven to the tops of mountains, I am compelled to explore these fragments of ancient landscape. Identifying ancient woods is a detective game: researchers study clues from old maps, and the woods themselves, to determine how old a forest is.

In Ireland, any wood that has survived since 1660 is considered ancient. Comprehensive mapping and surveying of the land only began in the 1650s, when the country was surveyed so it could be seized and planted following Cromwell's conquest. St Catherine's Wood appears on William Pretty's Down Survey map of 1655. After 1660, English landowners began planting new woods.

Some plants found at St Catherine's are indicators of ancient woodland too. The naturalist Robert Lloyd Praeger found one such flower here, the yellow bird's-nest, in the 1930s (though it has not been recorded since). Another indicator, the common toothwort, also occurs here. These species are usually only found in woods that have remained undisturbed for centuries.

Like all woods, May is the best time for wildflowers at St Catherine's. The rare and striking yellow archangel occurs here, as do other nationally important species like hairy St John's wort and green figwort. In Ireland

The old sluice gate on the Liffey (courtesy Ruth McNally)

old woods usually means oak, but there is not much of it at St Catherine's, where beech has largely displaced it. But other native trees thrive in different parts of the wood: ash, silver birch, hazel, holly, alder and willow. There are some yews too, and also invasive cherry laurel.

Follow the wide path through the woods under the steep embankment of glacial deposits. You can see the remains of an old millrace on your right, which once carried water to power mills.

The old weir and sluice gate are ahead on the river. Here the Liffey is squeezed through a funnel of white water, where kayakers play-boat in the rapids. Even the weir is rich in plant life, and you can see the roots of trees clinging to old stonework. The wide path ends up ahead, so turn sharply left and climb the trail into the woods.

Up here the ground drops so steeply it feels like walking through the canopy, and you can see the Liffey far below. 'This would be a good place to bring someone to declare your love for them,' my walking companion observed.

In March the woodland floor was a mosaic of greens, from lime to pine. Ferns sprouted from earth and trees, and I found a big fungus, the many-zoned polypore, emerging from a dead trunk. The only flower out was the white wood anemone, another indicator of old woods.

Emerging from the trees, cross the small footbridge and turn left to go back through the woods to the field you passed earlier. Continue straight back to the old lodge. From there, you can continue straight to meet a road. Follow it left onto an avenue and out to Leixlip. Or you can just return to the car park at Lucan.

Walking in the upper wood (courtesy Una McMahon)

THE GRAND CANAL

10/3/18
Walked to Hazel
hatch +
back

Lucan Road Bridge to Hazelhatch to Sallins
(Counties Dublin & Kildare)

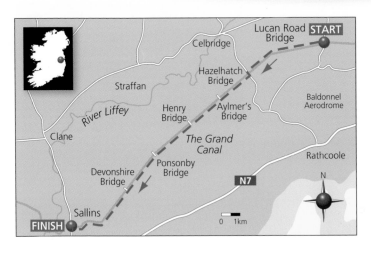

The lush wooded Grand Canal in west Dublin

Overview: Flat walking along the wooded towpath of the Grand Canal through rural Dublin and Kildare.

Trail: You are following the Grand Canal Way for the full walk.

Suitability: Flat and relatively easy walking on grassy towpaths, gravel tracks and quiet roads. The full route makes a long excursion.

Trailheads: Lucan Road Bridge, west Dublin. The bridge is located on the R120, which connects Lucan with Newcastle and Rathcoole. You can get onto the R120 at exit 4 of the N4, signposted for Lucan and Adamstown, and following the signs south for Newcastle and Adamstown. The bridge is about a 2km walk from Adamstown rail station.

Hazelhatch is on the R405 between Celbridge, County Kildare and Newcastle, County Dublin. Hazelhatch & Celbridge train station is a 600m walk by road from the bridge, heading north.

Finish: Sallins. The towpath of the canal leads you right into Sallins village. Turn left at the bridge in Sallins for the train station, where there are regular trains back to Dublin. Bus Éireann serves Sallins from Dublin.

Distance & time: Lucan Road Bridge to Hazelhatch is 4.5km, 1 to 1½ hours. Hazelhatch to Sallins is 12.5km, 3 to 4 hours.

Alternative routes: The full Grand Canal way runs from Dublin to the Shannon, so you can pick and choose which sections to walk.

Services: Full services in Sallins, at the end of the walk. Pub at Hazelhatch.

Map & further info: Trail map available from www.irishtrails.ie. Also the *Guide to the Grand Canal of Ireland* (Inland Waterways Association of Ireland). Online version at www.iwai.ie. OSi *Discovery Series* Sheets 49 and 50.

The towpath at Golierstown Bridge

Lucan Road Bridge to Hazelhatch

It is exhilarating to step onto a canal towpath in Dublin and know that, if you wanted, you could follow it across Ireland.

The Grand Canal Way runs beside the waterway from Dublin to the Shannon. One of the best stretches starts at Lucan Road Bridge in west Dublin. From here, follow the waymarkers west along the right bank. There is an old mill here where animal feed was once produced, and further on a lock house designed by canal engineer Thomas Omer.

The towpath is grassy and shaded by mature ash, sycamore and hawthorn. When I walked here in June, the high sun lit the clear water, and shoals of roach and rudd darted over the green water foliage. Every metre of the canal was full with fish.

I spotted a single white-clawed crayfish on the canal bottom. Ireland is a stronghold for this freshwater crustacean, which elsewhere in Europe is threatened by diseases introduced with North American crayfish. Thankfully, this alien species has not reached Ireland so far.

Work started on the Grand Canal at Clondalkin in 1756, more than forty years after the idea was proposed. It took twenty more years for the canal to get 21km to Sallins.

Soon you arrive at one of Omer's arched stone bridges. Past this, he directed the canal through limestone quarries, hoping to make transporting stone for building locks and bridges easier. But cutting through limestone proved an engineering headache. Water and vegetation has now reclaimed the old quarry.

Further ahead at Stacumney is another abandoned lock house, and the canal here is reassuringly wild, enclosed by woods and edged with reeds. Soon Hazelhatch Bridge appears in the distance, and the towpath drops you into the yard of McEvoy's pub.

On the water here you will find Dublin's most chaotic but inspiriting row of homes. Some of these barges are freshly painted and tidy, adorned with flowerpots. Others look abandoned and seem to be rotting into the canal bank. If you have had enough for one day, you can leave the canal here and catch a train at Hazelhatch & Celbridge station.

Hazelhatch to Sallins

Heading west from Hazelhatch Bridge, the Grand Canal Way switches to the left side of the channel. Now the towpath turns to gravel and the canal becomes more ordered. You pass Aylmer's Bridge and the towpath skirts the old Lyons Estate. With its cafe and restaurant, the Village at Lyons makes a good stop for refreshment (access up ahead by the lock, open weekends). This estate was once the home of the Cloncurrys. The second Lord Cloncurry was a director of the Grand Canal Company, and in its heyday this stretch of the canal had shops, a hotel, police barracks and a forge.

You come to the thirteenth lock (actually a double lock) and after that, the Henry Bridge at Ardclough. Bridges were typically named after local landowners who helped to finance the canal.

Just south of here is the ruined church and round tower at Oughterard, where Arthur Guinness is buried, and where Daniel O'Connell killed John

Cycling into Hazelhatch

D'Esterre in a pistol duel in 1815. D'Esterre was a member of Dublin Corporation who challenged O'Connell to the gunfight after O'Connell refused to apologise for criticising the corporation's treatment of Catholics.

There is an elegant old schoolhouse at Ardclough, built in 1839, and an overgrown quay that once served a nearby quarry. Past Ardclough you pass Ponsonby Bridge and the canal becomes wild again. The towpath returns to grass and the trees close in. Through gaps in the foliage you can look out to large, neat crop fields. Here I laid down on my backpack and rested my eyes in the close evening heat.

The towpath comes to Devonshire Bridge and, after that, two locks and a restored and extended lock cottage. Nearby, a channel cut from the River Morrell feeds the canal through a sluice gate. This small river, emptying into the canal, was Dublin city's main source of water until the Vartry Reservoir was built in 1869.

Soon you pass under a railway bridge and follow the tree-shaded towpath into Sallins, where more barges are moored. The canal engineer John Trail resigned here in 1777, having failed to complete the canal to the Liffey by then.

The Grand Canal opened for passenger traffic to Sallins two years later, while the Dublin city section was not finished until 1796. The canal reached the Shannon in 1804. However, the arrival of the railways killed the waterways. In 1852 passenger boats ceased, and in 1960 CIÉ withdrew its trade boats.

The Grand Canal near Sallins

THE GRAND CANAL

Milltown Feeder & Pollardstown Fen
(County Kildare)

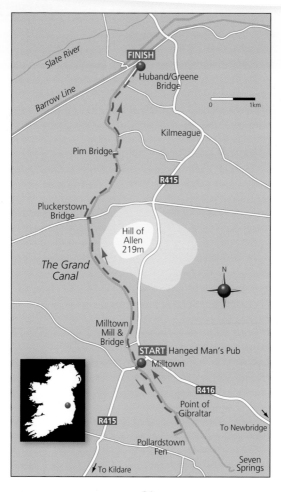

The old mill at Milltown

Overview: Flat walk on grassy and muddy towpaths, and quiet roads, along a little-used branch of the Grand Canal. Takes in a unique fen wetland.

Trail: No official trail but the towpath is walkable. Stick to the recommended sides of the channel to avoid dead ends or overgrown ground.

Suitability: Fairly easy walking, though moderately long, and quite muddy in places.

Trailheads: Milltown in County Kildare is 6.5km north of Kildare town on the R415 to Kilmeague, and is 6km north of Newbridge. Start from the Hanged Man's pub on the R415 (if coming from Newbridge, turn left by David's shop/Milltown Inn).

You can also start from Lowtown and walk the whole canal south. The feeder begins at the Huband/Greene Bridge on the Grand Canal, not far from Kilmeague and Robertstown.

Distance & time: Milltown to the Grand Canal at Lowtown is 8km one way, 2 to 2½ hours. Milltown to Pollardstown Fen is a 4km return trip, which should take about 1 to 1½ hours, but give yourself extra time to experience the wonderful fen fully.

Services: Shop and pub in Milltown. All services in Newbridge and Kildare town.

Map & further info: *Guide to the Grand Canal of Ireland* (Inland Waterways Association of Ireland), includes a map and guide to the Milltown Feeder. OSi *Discovery Series* Sheets 49 & 55.

Walking north on the feeder towards Pluckerstown

Near Lowtown, County Kildare, the Milltown Feeder quietly slips away from the Old Barrow Line of the Grand Canal under an odd bridge, marked on one side with '1788 Huband Bridge' and on the other with '1799 Greene Bridge'.

The feeder is a forgotten limb of the Grand Canal system, but an important one: it is a crucial water source for the whole canal, sucking from the freshwater springs at Pollardstown Fen. The feeder carried some freight and passengers too, but closed to navigation in 1945, though small boats can still use it.

From Milltown village, you can walk north along the feeder towards Lowtown or south into the wild fen. You can also walk the whole route south from Lowtown. But the scenery is best near Milltown – and there is a pub there too – so I think it makes for the best trailhead.

The landscape gets duller as you get closer to Lowtown, so a good outing would be to walk north from the Hanged Man's pub at Milltown and then turn back, leaving plenty of time to explore the fen once you get back to the pub.

Milltown to Lowtown

From the bridge at Milltown, follow the grassy towpath down behind the pub. Soon the seven-bay Milltown Mill rises ahead, beside an old cut-stone bridge. This scene is so still, it is hard to imagine that it once hummed with industry. There were mills nearby at Pluckerstown and Pollardstown, too.

Wooden footbridge on the Milltown Feeder

The spring water of the feeder is glass-clear, and in many places the canal bed is bright green with thick foliage. Continue on the right bank as the hedgerows recede and the canal emerges on an embankment into farmland. The wooded south face of the Hill of Allen rises ahead. This was, according to legend, the seat of Fionn mac Cumhaill and his Fianna, a legendary band of warriors.

The towpath turns into a farm track by some cattle sheds, and the big productive farmscapes of Kildare start to dominate, though there is some forestry and wilder pasture too.

The towpath joins a quiet road and brings you to the bridge at Pluckerstown. Cross over the bridge and follow the quiet road on the left bank of the canal, which brings you past pasture and a few houses. A deep quarry has scooped out much of the north and west faces of the Hill of Allen.

Soon more forestry appears on the left, and the canal quietens. You come to the elegant Pim's Bridge, the arch of which was graced by a statuesque heron when I approached in the November sun. There is an old limekiln in the wood-sheltered ruin beside the bridge. Cross the bridge to the right-hand side of the canal.

The Huband/Greene Bridge on the Grand Canal

The feeder emerges from the forestry and passes under a rustic timber footbridge. Further on, you join a quiet road that emerges onto the Huband/Greene Bridge, where the Milltown Feeder flows into the Old Barrow Line, spread-ing spring water from here through the whole Grand Canal system.

Milltown to Pollardstown Fen

From Milltown you can walk for about 2km south into the sprawling wetland of Pollardstown Fen. From the pub, cross the bridge (take care – the road is busy) and turn left on the wide grass path. The surrounding pasture starts to get rougher and wetter as you near the fen. Gradually the sedges, reeds and rushes take over, willows sprout from the damp, and wet woodland rises on your right. Though the canalside trees were almost bare when I walked here in November, I found the leaves of willow, elm, hazel and birch decaying in the trailside mulch.

Like bogs, fens occupy a borderland between solid and liquid. Fens are usually fed by groundwater, and are typically alkaline and nutrient rich. Bogs, on the other hand are rain fed, nutrient poor, and acidic. The calcium-rich springs of Pollardstown are fed by the Curragh aquifer to the south.

Walking into Pollardstown Fen

In the 1960s landowners began draining the fen – which formed after the last ice age – in order to farm the land. But there was a spirited campaign to save it, and the state eventually bought any land in private hands. In 1983, part of the fen was re-flooded to restore the wetlands.

The late sound-recording artist Tom Lawrence recorded a phenomenal variety of insect sounds underwater here for his wonderful work, *Water Beetles of Pollardstown Fen*. The naturalist Michael Viney, writing in *The Irish Times* in 2011, described this recording as, 'hypnotically alien, an endlessly varying chorus of clicks, chirrupings, churrs, buzzes and whines, pulsating and oscillating and sometimes of startling volume'.

The canal splits in two at a spot called the Point of Gibraltar. As I approached here, something large slunk under the water. Then at the canal's edge I found otter spraint, and one of the 'slides' these mammals use to enter the water. Throughout my walks along Ireland's canals I had desperately hoped to see an otter, but never did. This may have been the closest I got.

From the Point of Gibraltar, the left fork continues to the Seven Springs, a clear green spring-water pool. There are about forty springs in the fen. The grassy path follows the right fork instead, however, and soon goes right again at another fork in the channel. The wide path and the canal soon end, though another watery branch veers off to the left.

There are some faint tracks leading off from here, but ignore them and turn back to Milltown – walking out into the wet fen, where there are deep, overgrown drains, is not advised.

I lingered in this miniature wilderness for a bit before turning back. The fen seemed richer in life than most places I walked along the canals – birds rose from the reeds or scrub with each step, and winter congregations shifted across the sky. This wide, wet place seemed to glow as the rushes and reeds turned golden in the sinking November light.

THE GRAND CANAL

Tullamore to Pollagh to Ferbane
(County Offaly)

Shra Castle

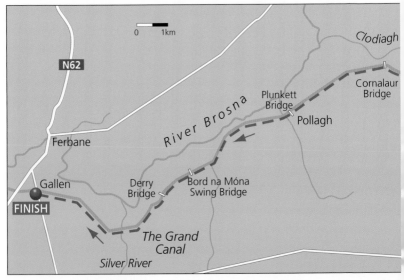

Overview: Flat along the towpath of the Grand Canal through pasture, forestry and peatlands.

Trail: You are following the Grand Canal Way for the full walk.

Suitability: The full route is a long and demanding day, even though the walking is flat. Probably best enjoyed by doing it in stages. Make sure to have plenty of daylight if doing the full route. The towpath surface varies from grassy to muddy to quiet roads.

Trailheads: Tullamore, County Offaly. Start from Kilbeggan Bridge on the Grand Canal at the bottom of Columcille St, which is an extension of High Street and Bridge Street. Tullamore is serviced by Irish Rail and by Bus Éireann, Kearns Transport (www.kearnstransport.com) and Slieve Bloom Coaches (www.slievebloomcoaches.ie).

Pollagh: Pollagh is located off the R436 between Ferbane and Clara. There is no public transport.

Finish: Gallen/Armstrong Bridge, or Ferbane, County Offaly. Ferbane is located 2km north of the bridge. From Ferbane, take the N62 towards Birr but turn left after 1km onto the R437 (signposted Kilcormac and Tullamore) for the bridge. From the bridge, Ferbane is signposted. Ferbane is serviced by Bus Éireann (Limerick–Athlone route).

Distance & time: Tullamore to Pollagh is 15.5km, 4 to 5 hours. Pollagh to Gallen is 10.5km (2½ to 3½ hours); it is a further 2km to Ferbane.

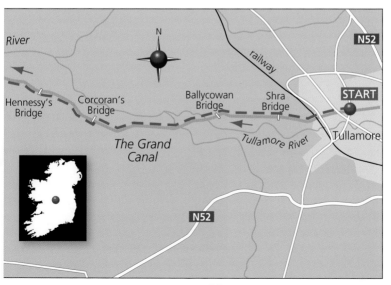

Shra Bridge on the Grand Canal

Services: All services in Tullamore. Pollagh has a shop a few hundred metres south of the canal. Ferbane has shops, pubs and food.

Alternative routes: The full Grand Canal way runs from Dublin to the Shannon, so you can pick and choose which sections to walk.

Map & further info: Trail maps from www.irishtrails.ie. Also the *Guide to the Grand Canal of Ireland* (Inland Waterways Association of Ireland). Online version at www.iwai.ie. OSi *Discovery Series* Sheets 48 (most of the walk) & 47.

Tullamore to Pollagh

Further west on the Grand Canal, tidy fields give way to rougher land. Towns grow scarcer and the land becomes bleaker but wilder.

Starting from bottom of Colmcille Street in Tullamore (beside Kelly's pub), cross the canal and turn left.

The Grand Canal reached Tullamore in 1798, but stalled while its backers debated how to bring it to the Shannon. It was eventually completed in 1803.

Tullamore harbour was once the site of warehouses and a canal hotel, but both were later demolished. The Tullamore Dew visitor centre is just across the canal as you set off.

Leaving the town you pass the twenty-seventh and twenty-eighth locks, and after going under the railway bridge,

Rushes along the Grand Canal

the ruins of Shra Castle are on your right. The Elizabethan officer John Briscoe built this tower house in 1588 after marrying into a local family.

About 3km further on, the five-storey facade of Ballycowan Castle looms ahead. The Huband Aqueduct lifts the canal over the Tullamore River, and gravity seems defeated as you and the canal are suspended above the river. 'I continue to be amazed at the how the canal was constructed through the wilderness of the midlands to such a standard by men with shovels and picks, horses and carts over 200 years ago,' Waterways Ireland engineer Louis Byrne told me. 'The bridges, locks and aqueducts are memorials to the skilled stonemasons but canal banks are memorials to the ordinary worker who may have laboured hard sixty to seventy hours a week just to survive.'

It was a real Irish spring day when I walked here: the sun warmed my back while an icy wind bit my cheeks. But I spotted a sign of warmer days ahead – a peacock butterfly on the towpath, coloured auburn, lilac and cream.

Eight kilometres from Tullamore the canal passes the Thatch Bar (on the far bank), and away to your right are the old churches at Rahan. Saint Carthage established a monastery here in the sixth century, and it became a hub of religious education. The original wooden churches are gone; the white stone church dates from the twelfth century and is still used by the Church of Ireland.

Just past the bar, follow the signs for the Grand Canal Way to cross over Corcoran's Bridge, to the left bank.

The Grand Canal Way remains on this side of the canal for the rest of this walk. For almost 6km between Hennessy's Bridge and Pollagh, the towpath is on a quiet road.

After the thirty-first lock at Cornalour, 12km into your walk, the landscape turns wilder. Walking here in March the blooming gorse gave away a secret: I had entered bog country. Farms yield to a hotchpotch of rough fields, scrub, forest and peatlands.

At Pollagh village, 15.5km from Tullamore, I stopped and rested by a bog-oak sculpture. The church here has an altar of bog oak too, and stained-glass windows by Harry Clarke Studios. Then the *Cheerful Lady* came by. I had been exchanging places in a race with this barge all day, but after Pollagh she forged ahead, and I never saw her again.

Pollagh to Ferbane

From Pollagh westwards the Grand Canal Way stays on the left bank of the channel. After 4.5km the towpath crosses a bog railway by a swing bridge. Bord Na Móna has one of the largest industrial rail networks in Europe, and rail cars once brought turf to nearby Ferbane Power Station, which was demolished in 2003.

Gravel towpath through bog, forest and pasture

The cutaway bogs are bleak and bare after decades of extraction, but as industrial harvesting ceases, wildlife is encroaching. Scrub and wood are reasserting themselves, forming another stratum on a landscape made more complex by its alternating layers of human and natural influence: bogs exploited then reclaimed by nature, fields cultivated then abandoned to scrub, cottages lived in then lost in the overgrowth.

In some places, nature is getting a leg-up. In 1991 Bord Na Móna flooded the cutaway peat fields at Turraun, just south of the canal, to create the first part of the Lough Boora Parklands. This restoration has created new habitats from old peatland. The parklands have birdwatching hides, angling lakes, bike hire and walking trails. You can visit the parklands on the R357 between Cloghan and Blueball (see www.loughboora.com for more information).

But I didn't have time for that. As I walked westward the rain hit my face and the sky blackened. The canal may be man-made, but when you are crossing the bare bog far from anywhere it is bleakly wild.

Beyond Derry Bridge, the Macartney Aqueduct, 7.5km from Pollagh, brings you over the Silver River. Past here the towpath joins a quiet road. This walk ends 3km further on at the next bridge in Gallen. You could arrange transport from here, or walk 2km by road to Ferbane to catch a bus. Shannon Harbour, where the canal ends and meets the Shannon, is 9.5km further west on the canal.

Towards Gallen in early spring

THE ROYAL CANAL

Enfield to Kilcock
(Counties Meath & Kildare)

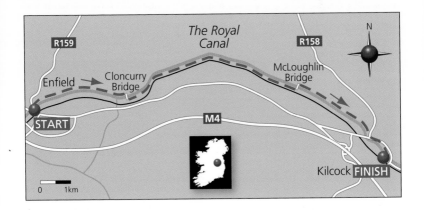

The Royal Canal curving towards Kilcock

Overview: Half day's walk along the flat grassy towpath of the Royal Canal through rural Meath and Kildare.

Trail: You are following the Royal Canal Way for the duration of the walk.

Suitability: The route is fairly flat and easy and on mostly grassy surfaces, with a little walking on quiet roads.

Start: Enfield is in the very south of County Meath, just off exit 9 on the M4. You can join the canal at the west end of the town, by the train station. Enfield is serviced by Irish Rail on the Dublin–Sligo Line, and by Bus Éireann and Citylink.

Finish: Kilcock is on the R148 just off exit 8 on the M4. Kilcock train station is beside Shaw's Bridge on the canal. Kilcock is on the Dublin–Sligo rail line, and is also serviced by Bus Éireann (Dublin–Mullingar route).

Distance & time: 13km, 3 to 4 hours.

Alternative routes: The Dublin–Sligo train also stops along the canal at Maynooth, 6km east of Kilcock, and Leixlip, another 6km east again, allowing you to extend the walk easily and make use of the train connections. Further west the Royal Canal Way is less accessible by rail, with the exception of Mullingar. A walking and cycling greenway has recently been opened along the Longford Branch of the canal from Longford to Cloonsheerin (8.5km), and along the man line of the canal from Cloonsheerin to the Shannon at Cloondara (7.5km). The full Royal Canal Way runs for 144km from Dublin to the Shannon.

Services: Shops, pubs, food and supermarkets at Enfield and Kilcock.

Maps & further info: Trail maps available to download from www.irishtrails. ie. Also the *Guide to the Royal Canal of Ireland* (Inland Waterways Association of Ireland). The area is covered by OSi *Discovery Series* Sheet 49.

I n the 1750s, two canal routes from Dublin to the Shannon were proposed. The more southerly option was chosen, and this became the Grand Canal. However, canal lore says that in 1789 a disgruntled Grand Canal director stormed out of a meeting, vowing to build a rival waterway. The Royal Canal Company was formed, resurrecting plans for a more northerly route to the Shannon.

The Royal Canal was completed in 1817, and in 1845 the Midland Great Western Railway bought the entire waterway to build a rail line beside it. This turned out to be great for modern walkers, because you can easily get off the train at one station and walk to the next.

Perhaps the best stretch for this is between Enfield and Kilcock. From Enfield, join the Royal Canal Way at the western end of the town, on the same side of the road as the train station. The towpath here is grassy and shaded by mature sycamore, ash, beech and oak.

When I walked here in late summer, the canal was coloured by wildflowers on the water, bank and towpath: yellow water-lilies, white bindweed, red clover, purple field scabious, purple loosestrife, white-and-yellow eyebright. The common reeds along the water-fringe bore purple flowers, crickets rattled from the grass, while butterflies floated above the motionless water. This was a world away from when I last walked the Royal Canal, in the dead of January. Then, the water had a coat of cellophane-thin ice, and I daydreamed of skating down the channel rather than walking beside it.

Before work began on the Royal, the Grand Canal Company suggested both projects save money by partially sharing a route, but the Royal

Wildflowers on the towpath

Looking east from Cloncurry Bridge

rejected the idea. The engineers struggled with sinking of the channel and slippage of the banks on this section. The route had not been thoroughly surveyed in advance and construction paused just west of Enfield in 1800 when the company ran out of funds.

The towpath joins a quiet road, and about 3 km from Enfield you reach Cloncurry Bridge. Cross to the right-hand side of the canal here. The towpath turns grassy again.

Canal walking is the opposite of hillwalking. When climbing a mountain you have to navigate carefully, watch the terrain, study the weather. But canal walking is thoughtless: the towpath is flat, your bearing is straight and your mind can wander. The only thing that might disturb your peace here is the occasional train coming by on the Dublin–Sligo line, which runs right beside the canal. In places the railway is just beyond the hedgerow to your right; in other parts, rough meadows fill the forgotten land between you and the track.

Towpath along the Royal Canal

There is a quiet road on the far bank; after it ends by old farm buildings, the canal grows into its wild best. It passes woodland where birch overhangs the water, and then the land opens up around you again. The fields seem to get bigger and tidier the further east you go and the hedgerows more ordered.

There are long straight sections of canal here, which can be tiring to the eye, but the 6km after Cloncurry Bridge is still wild, lush and remote.

Next you come to Fern's Lock (a double lock) and McLoughlin Bridge. This is the first lock on the walk: the entire stretch from here to Thomastown, County Westmeath, 23km west of Enfield, is a 'long level' with no locks.

Woodland between Cloncurry Bridge and Fern's Lock

The Royal Canal Way switches back to the left bank of the canal at McLoughlin Bridge. Further on there is a large warehouse across the canal, and the towpath crosses a timber footbridge. Then you come to Allen (or Spin) Bridge, where the old bridge is now encased in a more modern structure.

You are pretty much in Kilcock now, but the town is hidden by foliage. But soon you arrive at Shaw's Bridge and the sixteenth lock, near Kilcock train station.

The canal arrived here in 1796, but it took another twenty-one years to reach the Shannon. By then the Royal Canal Company had dissolved and the state controlled the waterway. The Grand Canal had heaped pressure on its rival by insisting the Royal take the longer route set out in its charter, rather than meet the Shannon at Lough Ree.

Cattle grazing canalside pasture

The Royal Canal ended up costing £1.4m to build, compared to £877,000 for the Grand, and never saw as much traffic, either. Like all Ireland's waterways it declined in the era of trains and then roads. There was a brief revival of horse-drawn traffic on the canals during the Second World War. But the last independent trader on the Royal retired in 1951, and the channel grew derelict.

The Royal Canal Amenity Group was formed in the 1970s, hoping to save the canal. Stretch by stretch, the waterway was restored, and in 2010 the Royal Canal joined with the Shannon for a second time.

Spin Bridge on the Royal Canal

THE ROYAL CANAL

Mullingar to Ballynacargy
(County Westmeath)

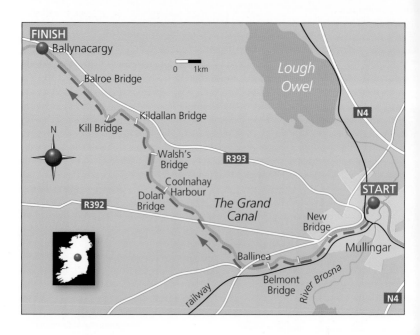

Jogging beside the Royal Canal near Ballinea

Overview: Flat towpath walk through the farmed landscape of rural Westmeath.

Trail: You are following the Royal Canal Way for the full walk (also the Westmeath Way from Mullingar to Belmont Bridge).

Suitability: Easy walking though the full 19km is fairly long. Mullingar to Coolnahay is ideal for cyclists too.

Trailheads: Mullingar, County Westmeath. Start from Scanlan's Bridge on Harbour Street (an extension of Castle Street) on the north side of the town. Mullingar is well serviced by Irish Rail and Bus Éireann.

Coolnahay Harbour. On the L1804 road, which can accessed from either the R392 (Mullingar to Ballymahon) or the R393 (Mullingar to Longford). No public transport here.

Ballynacargy is on the R393 (Mullingar to Longford) about 15.5km west of Mullingar. Bus Éireann serviced Ballynacargy on Fridays only at the time of writing.

Distance & time: Mullingar to Coolnahay is 10.5km, 2½ to 3½ hours. Coolnahay to Ballynargy is 8km, 2 to 3 hours.

Services: All services in Mullingar. Tea room at Coolnahay open seasonally. Shop and pubs at Ballynacargy.

Alternative routes: The full Royal Canal way runs for 144km from Dublin to the Shannon, so you can pick and choose which sections to walk.

Map & further info: Trail maps from www.irishtrails.ie. Also the *Guide to the Royal Canal of Ireland* (Inland Waterways Association of Ireland). Online version at www.iwai.ie. OSi *Discovery Series* Sheet 41.

Mullingar to Coolnahay

Further west, the only train stop on the main line of the Royal Canal is at Mullingar, so you cannot walk from one station to the next as between Enfield, Kilcock, Maynooth and Leixlip. But Westmeath's county town is still a good place to explore the canal. You must either walk out-and-back, or arrange transport from the far end of your hike.

The Royal Canal reached Mullingar in 1806, sixteen years after construction began. The land surveyor John Brownrigg said Lough Owel, north of the town, would provide the waterway with 'a more abundant supply of pure spring water than any inland navigation this side of China'. Lough Owel is still one of the canal's main feeders.

Start from Scanlan's Bridge, which divides an old harbour in two. Go west along the left-hand bank of the canal. The towpath all the way from here to Coolnahay is fairly smooth, suitable for cycling as well as walking. Mullingar's original canal harbour was further east, in an area once 'somewhat notorious for the number of shebeens and dance houses it contained', according to local historian Ruth Illingworth.

The late-nineteenth-century Loretto Convent, built in Gothic style, is across the channel, while the grounds of the Cathedral of Christ the King are on your left. But until it escapes the town the canal is fairly charmless, so power on ahead. You go under an ugly rail bridge, cross over Dominick Street (stay on the left bank), and pass the train station. Further ahead on your left is a terrace of railway houses and an old rail warehouse. Damp scrub fills the spaces between the canal, the railway and the industrial estates.

The original journey time from Dublin to Mullingar by canal was twelve hours. This was cut to eight hours with the launch of the faster 'flyboats' in 1833. Food and alcohol were served on board, and there were sometimes riotous and drunken scenes whenever emigrants departed. Provisions were also sent up the canal by boat during the Famine, with military escort. But the Dublin railway reached Mullingar in 1848, and passenger traffic on the canal soon ended, though freight transport continued.

The Dublin–Sligo railway hugs the waterway, and you soon go under another road bridge. Fields and hedgerows start to form as the suburban fades to the rural, with the canal raised high on an embankment.

When I walked here in November the sky was a bright grey-white, and the pale sun had yet to burn off the morning fog, so no blue broke through. But the canal was still full with deep colour: wheaten reeds, yellow bramble leaves, red holly berries and the milky-green water.

The towpath goes under Kilpatrick Brige, then comes to Belmont Bridge. Cross to the right (north) side of the canal here and carry on to the harbour at Ballinea, 6km from Mullingar. Cross the first, older bridge back to the left bank of the canal, and follow the Royal Canal Way down under

Belmont Bridge on the Royal Canal

the newer road bridge. The old bridge is one of only two 'skew bridges' – which do not cross the waterway at a right angle – on the Royal Canal.

The railway leaves the canal, the roads recede and the waterway quietens. To the right the towpath looks out to smooth, undulating pasture, while on your left there is rougher land and forestry. The towpath goes under two bridges at Shandonagh as the canal grows remoter still.

You arrive to Coolnahay Harbour, 10.5km from Mullingar. There is a picnic area on the far bank, while tea and refreshments are served from the lock cottage in season. The lock here marks the western end of the Royal Canal's 15km summit level – its highest stretch – which starts at the twenty-fifth lock, east of Mullingar. The canal reached Coolnahay in 1809.

Coolnahay to Ballynacargy

Continue on the left bank from the bridge at Coolnahay. When I walked here, the towpath turned into a rougher track. But Westmeath County Council had plans to develop a smoother cycling and walking path here, and this may be complete by the time you visit. These harder surfaces are springing up all along Ireland's waterways – the contentious plan to 'pave' the Barrow Way in County Carlow is a case in point.

After much investment to restore them, Ireland's waterways are still underused, and if paving the towpaths brings

The canal becomes quieter and more isolated near Coolnahay

more people out, that is a good thing. But I prefer grassy towpaths as they make the canal feel wilder and are a rich refuge for wildflowers. The canals are already walkable and cyclable: they just require sturdier footwear or a stronger bike in places.

The Royal Canal Way stays on the left side of the canal for the rest of the walk. Past Coolnahay, I watched a group of donkeys and ponies graze the grassy towpath on the far bank.

You pass the twenty-seventh and twenty-eighth locks as the landscape becomes more textured, a plaid pattern of lumpen hills, lawn-like fields, rough pasture, and damp grassland. The towpath goes under Walsh's Bridge, then Kildallan Bridge. When I passed here the clouds closed

over and sealed away the sun, and the sky became a marbled blue-grey. The canal water slowly turned to mercury in the declining afternoon light.

Beyond Kildallan Bridge, you pass the twenty-ninth, thirtieth and thirty-first locks in quick succession – each with its own lock cottage. Walking here, my footfall rose a snipe from the canalside grasses.

The lock cottage at Coolnahay

Soon you pass Kill Bridge, now used only by farmers, and forestry rises on both sides of the waterway. Then you come to the next bridge at Balroe. Continuing on the left bank it is 2km further to Ballynacargy. Just before the village are the ruins of an old three-bay canal hotel. Ballynacargy owes much of its development as a village to the arrival of the canal in the early nineteenth century.

Kill Bridge on the Royal Canal

THE BOYNE

Boyne Ramparts Walk, Navan to Stackallen
(County Meath)

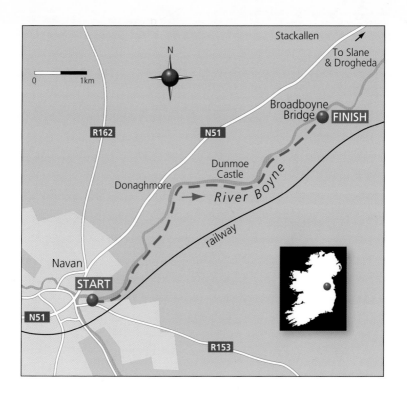

Cattle grazing by the Boyne (courtesy Una McMahon)

Overview: Flat walk on the grassy towpath between the River Boyne and its canal through an area rich in human heritage.

Trail: You are following the Boyne Ramparts Walk. This is a linear walk with no turns or navigation needed. You will either need to arrange transport from Broadboyne Bridge, or walk back from there to Navan.

Suitability: Flat and fairly easy walking on a grassy surface. You may encounter livestock.

Start: Ramparts car park. From Navan town centre, take the R153 (signposted for Duleek and Ashbourne), crossing over the Boyne. The car park is about 250m past the bridge on the left-hand side. Both Bus Éireann and Sillian Coaches serve Navan.

Finish: Broadboyne Bridge, Stackallen, is off the N51 between Navan and Slane (turn onto the L3411 at Wiggers Cross, signposted for Ardmulchan).

Distance & time: 6.5km one way (1½ to 2½ hours), 13km return (3½ to 4½ hours).

Alternative routes: There are plans to open waks on the Boyne down-stream from Stackallen to Slane, and between Oldbridge and Newgrange.

Services: All services in Navan, none at Stackallen.

Map & further info: OSi *Discovery Series* Sheet 42 covers the area but not does not show this trail in detail. Map not essential as no navigation is required. The Boyne Navigation is currently being restored by the Boyne branch of the IWAI (www.boyne.iwai.ie) under the direction of An Taisce.

More than any Irish river, the Boyne is wrapped in myth and mystery. This valley is lined with ancient landmarks: the prehistoric monuments at Newgrange, Knowth, Dowth and the Hill of Tara, twelfth-century Trim Castle, and the site of the Battle of the Boyne. Legend says the river was created when the Celtic goddess Boann

The wooded Boyne Ramparts Walk (courtesy Una McMahon)

approached a sacred well, causing its waters to rise up and flow towards the sea. And it was from this river that Fionn mac Cumhaill tasted the Salmon of Knowledge and gained the wisdom of the world.

The best place for a long walk by the Boyne is Navan. From here you can follow the river and its canal for 6.5km through neat countryside. Between 1748 and 1800 canals were built to make the Boyne navigable for trade. This walk follows the old towpath.

Boats once carried timber, coal and wheat upstream, with oats, barley, flour, linen and yarn going down to the sea at Drogheda. After trade declined, steamboats carried sightseers on the river. But competition from rail killed the canal and it was abandoned in 1923. An Taisce bought the waterway in 1969, and its seaward end at Drogheda is being restored.

Setting off near Ruxton's Bridge in the early autumn, I followed the towpath through reddening woods that felt more like Appalachia than Ireland. Green chlorophyll in the leaves decayed; yellow and orange took over. The trees here are tall and various: oaks, ash, sycamore, horse chestnut, pine, spruce.

You come to Athlumney weir – the first of many on this walk – and canal bridge, and later to Rowley's Lock and derelict lock house. Rowley was a local landowner and one of the canal's main funders. Look out for the small plaque on the bridge commemorating both him and the canal engineer Richard Evans. The ancient single-arch remains of Babes Bridge, which dates from the twelfth century, are ahead on the river. Named for the Norman landowner John le Baub, this was apparently the

Swans on the Boyne (courtesy Una McMahon)

only bridge on the Boyne to survive a violent flood in 1330.

I watched a heron fish by a weir and later my footfall sent a moorhen scurrying from the canal. Beside the path the gnarled oaks were laden with acorns, the ash leaves were turning lemon yellow, and I picked conkers from the horse chestnuts.

Looking over the Boyne near Stackallen (courtesy Una McMahon)

Dunmoe Castle, which probably dates from the late fourteenth or early fifteenth century, appears across the river. Cromwell is said to have fired a single cannonball at it before carrying on his murderous way. Legend says a tunnel leads under the river to the castle, which was destroyed by fire in 1799. The ruins of a medieval church are near the castle. Below it on the riverbank is a mill that was active until the First World War.

Ardmulchan House will soon startle you through the foliage on your right. This red-brick manor was built at the start of twentieth century and is privately owned. Past the house above the river are the Norman ruins of Ardmulchan Church. The church was built on even older foundations and there is an ancient graveyard beside it.

William Wilde's book *The Beauties of the Boyne, and its Tributary, the Blackwater* says that an alliance of Vikings and Leinstermen defeated the family of the southern Uí Néil in battle here in 968. The church bells were thrown into the river during the Reformation to save them from plunderers, according to legend.

Walking here, I daydreamed that I might see a Boyne currach on the river. These traditional oval vessels were constructed from woven hazel rods and animal hide. The currach builder and artist Claidhbh Ó Gibne, along with the Boyne Currach Heritage Group, is reviving this local craft.

Past Ardmulchan Church you come to Taafe's Lock, and then the towpath leaves the riverbank. You can still see the wide, smooth Boyne from across the fields.

Soon you arrive at Broadboyne Bridge, designed by Richard Evans in the 1820s. It was once customary to take animals across the river here to fend off diseases and fairies.

THE BARROW

Old Mill Loop, Glenbarrow
(County Laois)

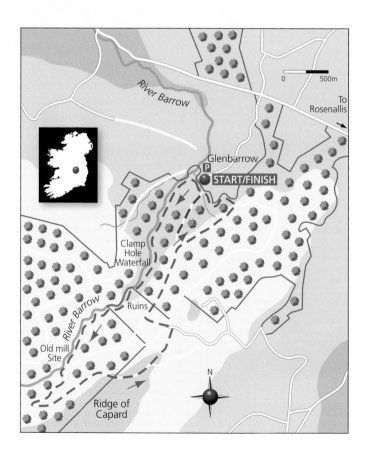

Overview: Invigorating looped hike up the wooded gorge of the young Barrow and a mountain boardwalk, followed by a descent on forestry roads.

Trail: You are following the red arrows of the Old Mill Loop.

Suitability: Graded strenuous. Follows very rough forest trails, boardwalks, and forest roads. There is a good bit of climbing, some minor scrambles and slippery ground. The trail enters reasonably high and remote terrain.

Trailhead: Glenbarrow is near the village of Rosenallis, County Laois, which is on the R422 between Clonaslee and Mountmellick. Follow the signpost from the village, turning right after 1.5km and then left 2km further on at a crossroads.

Distance & time: 10km (3 to 4 hours).

Alternative routes: There are shorter looped trails at Glenbarrow, including the Eco Walk, which includes numbered stops and a guide available at www. slievebloom.ie.

Maps & further info: Trail maps and more info available at www. coillteoutdoors.ie and www.slievebloom.ie. The area is covered by OSi *Discovery Series* Sheet 54. Some maps show older versions of the loop.

At the time of writing, some maps showed the trail crossing the river to the right bank after leaving the car park, then crossing back over further on. These footbridges were removed after a landslide, so the trail now continues on the left bank of the Barrow all the way up.

Clamp Hole waterfall

The Barrow rises in Laois. It flows north from the Slieve Bloom Mountains before turning 180 degrees and heading south for the sea at Waterford. The river's headwaters at Glenbarrow are one of the few places in Ireland where you can walk a wooded valley high into hills. There are various looped trails here, but the Old Mill Loop (red arrows) brings you highest up the valley. It was here that I witnessed the most terrible example of a river's power that I have ever seen.

From the car park, follow the red arrows down a sunken lane. You will come to a wooden gate and enter Glenbarrow forest through spruces, a good spot for fungus hunting in autumn. It was high summer when I visited, when the river was only a dribble navigating through boulders.

The young Barrow (courtesy Ann Lannigan)

After you pass a wooden hut, the trail turns rougher. Expect small scrambles, slippery rock and uneven ground. The trail crosses Old Red Sandstone, formed from sand deposited at the mouth of an ancient river over 300 million years ago. This is the floor of an old quarry. Look for small holes in which explosives were placed for blasting the rock. Near the hut on the river cliff there are initials carved by the men who worked here.

Climbing the Old Mill Loop by Clamp Hole Waterfall

Soon you come to Clamp Hole Waterfall, which formed as the river eroded softer mudstones under the sandstone. The sandstone could no longer support itself so it collapsed, creating the falls. You can view the falls from the railings, but at full volume the river can violently flood the path here, so if necessary you can also follow the arrows up through the trees to your left.

The trail climbs sharply, and there are steep, unguarded drops to your right. These are cliffs of moraine, deposited by glaciers and now colonised by willow, birch, oak, rowan and holly. Old maps are marked upstream of the waterfall with the words 'hermit's cell', but no sign of this mysterious structure remains.

The combined effect of wood and gorge here is invigorating, and each step is a revelation. In late spring and early summer, look out for wildflowers like bluebell, wood sanicle, primrose, wild garlic and dog violet.

The Waterfall Loop (blue route) soon turns left up steps. But to continue on the Old Mill Loop, go right over a small stream and follow the red arrows up the valley. There are signs of old farmsteads ahead, remnants of when this high remote valley was inhabited.

Rough and steep steps on the Old Mill Loop

Deep down in the trees, it is easy to imagine this wood might go on forever. But the wonderful shock of this high, wooded valley dissipates when, on leaving it, you realise how small it is amid the surrounding mountains.

The trail emerges from the trees into heath and clear-felled forestry. Ignore the footbridge for the Slieve Bloom Way and stay on the left bank of the river. Keep with the red arrows as the orange trail leaves the river. There is an old millstone up ahead by the site of an old mill, and almost 300m up, the Barrow's banks are still wooded with oak, holly, birch and hazel.

The trail turns left and climbs up to a forest road. It then goes right and the red arrows direct you up to a boardwalk through thick heather and on to a viewing point at the Ridge of Capard. From here, follow the red arrows straight down through the car park and on a trail into the forest. You then turn right on a forest road, and when you reach a fork, either keep straight for the car park, or veer right for a longer route back that will take you on a boardwalk into mixed woods.

The night of my visit to Glenbarrow, I camped in a high grove of hazel. It started to rain that evening, and did not stop during the night or the next morning. Overnight, the young Barrow turned from a low dribble to a raging peat-brown froth that had started to break its banks. I stepped onto the wooden Slieve Bloom Way footbridge warily, staring down into this foam and fury. Overnight, forest streams

Waterfall on the Glenbarrow gorge

58

The young Barrow in the Slieve Bloom Mountains

had turned into miniature torrents, and at Clamp Hole waterfall the river violently flooded the path. Back in the spruce wood near the car park, a waterfall had formed overnight.

I later read in John Feehan's book, *The Landscape of Slieve Bloom*, that the word Barrow may have come from the Irish *beir*, meaning to boil. Feehan also recounts a legend which says that anyone who looks into the river's headwaters will unleash torrential downpours on these hills. Had I ventured a little too close to this river's source?

The Barrow in spate after heavy rain

THE CLODIAGH

Brittas Loop, Clonaslee
(County Laois)

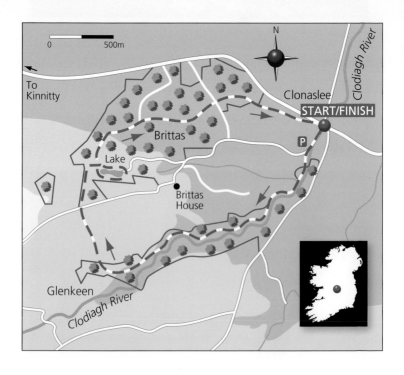

The Clodiagh River at Clonaslee

Overview: Looped walk that first follows the wooded Clodiagh River, then joins a farm lane before winding through mixed woodland and past a small man-made lake.

Trail: You are following the blue waymarkers of the Brittas Loop for the full walk.

Suitability: The trail grade is moderate. It follows forest tracks, grassy lanes and rough woodland trails.

Trailhead: Clonaslee is located on the R422, 14.5km west of Mountmellick, County Laois. From M. D. Hickey's pub at the crossroads, cross the road and follow the river. The trailhead is just ahead on your left. Martleys serves Clonaslee on its daily Dublin–Portlaoise service (www.martleys.com).

Distance & time: 6.5km, 2 to 2½ hours.

Alternative routes: You can also cross the footbridges over the Clodiagh River to explore the small section of woodland on the opposite bank. The Slieve Bloom Way also passes through this valley.

Services: Shops, pubs and cafe in Clonaslee.

Map & further info: Trail maps and info from www.coillteoutdoors.ie and www.slievebloom.ie. The area is covered by OSi *Discovery Series* Sheet 54.

Footbridge over the Clodiagh

The Slieve Bloom Mountains are famous for the blanket bog of their high plateau. From the high bog, a series of rivers radiates down through forested valleys. The Clodiagh is one of these rivers, rising on Knockachoora and descending through mixed woodland about the village of Clonaslee.

From the trailhead, the Brittas Loop follows the river upstream. Follow the blue waymarkers left into the forest. The trail follows the river southwest through woods. The name Clodiagh is most likely derived from the Irish *cloddagh*, meaning 'stony stream'.

In spring, keep an eye out for the wood anemone and lesser celandine here; in May for bluebells. I visited in mid-August when birch leaves were yellowing, blackberries ripening and the bracken beginning to rust.

The trail ascends the river valley for almost 3km, crossing many stiles. The enclosed areas near the river allow livestock from neighbouring fields to come and drink.

You will pass weirs and the ruins of a bridge, where beech trees cling to the stonework. The trail passes footbridges too, but stay on the right

Farm lane on the Brittas Loop

Into Brittas Woods

bank. There is a lot of hazel and beech here, with ash and Douglas fir too.

The trail leaves the river, climbs upwards, and follows a grassy lane past hawthorn, rowan and some birch. You soon emerge onto a quiet road. Turn right here, then immediately left to follow the blue waymarkers onto a narrow track through beech and holly.

The path winds through the wood to a grove of Scots pine, a graceful tree deeply rooted in Ireland's ecological past. Scots pine once flourished in our mountains and lowlands, thriving on marginal soils, but declined as Ireland's climate got wetter and early farmers cleared the land. There is debate about whether it became extinct here or survived in isolated refuges. However, most Scots pine here today has been reintroduced from Scotland, where fragments of ancient highland forest survive.

Soon the trail arrives at Brittas Lake, which was built as a reservoir for the Brittas Estate. It has picnic benches and old fishing stands along its banks. Nearby Brittas House (which is not on the trail) was built in 1869 by General Francis Plunkett Dunne, the local landowner. It was designed in Gothic style by the architect John McCurdy. Irish Republican Army soldiers hid in the house during the 1922 Civil War, but were discovered by Free State forces. Most fled through the woods, and one solider was shot and killed.

The waymarkers at the lake can be confusing, but essentially they direct you on a complete loop of the lake. Then, as you leave it behind, rather than turn left down the

Brittas Lake

63

track on which you came through the wood, continue straight. At the barriers go left onto a forest road.

There was once a large oak wood here, but it was mostly cleared in the 1940s and replaced with conifers. But you can still see old oaks along the track. The trail goes right at the first fork in the road, then left where a grassy path leads right. When you come to a barrier, cross the road and carry on straight down a grassy lane.

Here, in the sinking evening light, I watched a fallow deer and her fawn graze the track. I expected them to bolt, but the mother went into the trees, leaving the fawn behind to stare at me. I walked on, but before I could get any closer the mother returned and saw me, and both deer darted off.

All day I had been looking for signs of wild boar, a species once hunted to extinction in Ireland. But now, whether through farm escapes or illegal releases, it has reappeared, and one boar was shot near Clonaslee in 2011.

You eventually emerge from the wood down a scrubby green lane to an old gate of the Brittas Estate, on the west side of Clonaslee village. Carry on straight past the houses to the crossroads by the river, where you turn right for the trailhead.

The green lane leading back to Clonaslee

THE SILVER RIVER

Paul's Lane Loop
& The Offaly Way
(County Offaly)

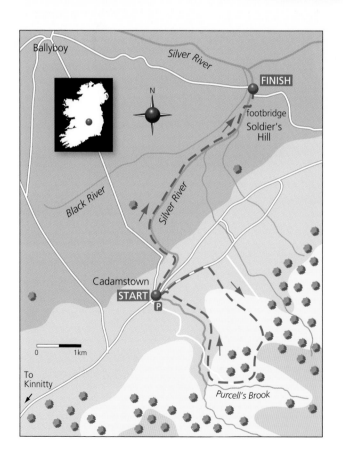

Overview: This walk combines two trails to explore the Silver River, first down a wooded ravine, then along the edges of farmland and forestry.

Trail: Start by completing Paul's Lane Loop (blue arrows), and once back at the trailhead, follow the Offaly Way down a linear riverside trail.

Suitability: The Paul's Lane Loop includes some steep ascending and descending on rough and wet trails. The Offaly Way section is flat and relatively easy terrain, but you may encounter livestock.

Trailhead: Dempsey's pub, Cadamstown, County Offaly. The village is on the R421, 3km northeast of Kinnity, County Offaly. There is no public transport here.

Distance & time: Paul's Lane Loop is 5km, about 1½ to 2½ hours. From the trailhead to the footbridge on the Offaly Way is 6km one way (2 to 2½ hours) or 12km return (3 to 4 hours). You can continue from the footbridge to a quiet road if you can arrange transport from there, making for a one-way walk of 6.5km from Cadamstown.

Alternative routes: There are various other loops marked at Cadamstown. For a linear walk, when the Offaly Way emerges onto the road at the end of this walk it continues by road for a while and then rejoins the Silver River again before coming to Kilcormac.

Services: Pub at Cadamstown. Kinnity and Clonaslee are larger villages nearby with shops and pubs.

Map & further info: You can download trail maps at www.irishtrails.ie and www.slievebloom.ie. The area is covered by OSi *Discovery Series* Map 54.

The Silver River descends from the Slieve Bloom Mountains to the pleasant village of Cadamstown, flowing down a wooded gorge and out across farmland. Two ancient roads, the *Slí Dála* ('the way to the assembly') and the *Slí Mór* ('the great highway', which runs along the ridge of the Esker Riada) once met at the abbey of Leitir Lugna nearby, but little trace of the abbey remains.

There is a small garden by the trailhead with stone inscriptions that commemorate local victims of the Famine and Cadamstown men who died during the 1798 Rebellion. The Ballykelly Stone, an old pagan fertility stone, is here too.

Leave the river and follow Paul's Lane Loop up the road behind Dempsey's pub, where cottages cluster. Even though the road is quiet, this is still an 80km/h zone, so take care. After 750m the trail turns right up an old lane.

This is Paul's Lane, and I don't know if it meets any strict definition, but it certainly feels like a *holloway* – a sunken pathway lower than the

Paul's Lane

land around it, eroded into soft rock by a long history of use. The writer Robert MacFarlane describes holloways as a 'sunken labyrinth of wildness' in his book *The Wild Places*. He compares holloways to creases on a hand, a product of wear. 'Trodden by innumerable feet, cut by innumerable wheels, they are the records of journeys to market, to worship, to sea,' he writes.

A friend once told me how, after coming back from arid Western Australia, he noticed that in Ireland botanic life sprouts from every habitable crevice. Paul's Lane is the physical embodiment of this idea, lush and wooded, and bordered by stone walls buried under thick foliage and moss. I walked here on a September evening as the sun dipped behind the hazel, hawthorn and ash.

Stick to the left of the lane as you climb: the right side is a slippery drain. Higher up, the trees recede and gorse encroaches. You pass a cluster of ruined cottages colonised by beech, ash, hawthorn and fuchsia. This is the abandoned village of Bordingstown, which dates from the eighteenth century, and was once the site of a hospital. Paul's Lane is named for Bordingstown's last resident, Paul Maher, who died in 1900.

At the junction with the signposts, follow the blue arrows right on the gorse-lined track. The trail goes down through forestry and past a rusty gate, and soon descends sharply. My walking buddy pointed out deer tracks in the muck here, and moments later we looked down a firebreak and saw a fallow deer looking back.

Weir on the Silver River

Wooded lane by the Silver River

The trail joins Purcell's Brook, a ravine thickly wooded with hazel, willow, hawthorn and birch, then arrives at the sandy banks of the Silver River, following it downstream past a tall weir. You cross a series of stiles and descend through woods so green and damp they feel like rainforest. The trail is rough, with worn-out steps, rocky ledges and bulging roots. There is a lot of hazel by the trail, with some rangy oaks above. We found a brilliant purple mushroom, the amethyst deceiver, under ferns.

In his book *At the Foot of Slieve Bloom: History and Folklore of Cadamstown*, local historian Paddy Heaney recalls the pools of the upper Silver River system being full with trout in his youth. He writes of going back to old fishing holes in later years and finding none. One pool on the river is named Clutterbuck's Hole, after a man who was murdered and dumped in the river, after being gifted land seized from local tenants.

You pass a side trail leading to a viewing point on the river, and further down come to a small waterfall. The rivers of Slieve Bloom formed after the last ice age, when raging meltwater cut through soft glacial deposits and into the rocks below. Like Glenbarrow (Route 9), this gorge exposes the Old Red Sandstone beneath. Upstream, the tilting of the earth's plates has also thrust older Silurian rock to the surface.

The trail emerges onto a farm lane, which descends back to Dempsey's pub. To keep walking the river, cross the bridge and follow the Offaly Way sign across the road. The next part of the walk is linear, so you will either have to retrace your steps, or leave a car at the other end. The trail passes an old corn mill, which dates from 1831 and was built with stone taken from the abbey at Leitir Lugna.

The trail goes through the yard of the mill house, then up steps and through a gate. You join the Silver River through beech woods and then pass the ancient Ardara Bridge. The bridge was sealed off for restoration work when I went by, but we saw a red squirrel on the scaffolding.

Further on there was fresh pine marten scat on the trail. Slieve Bloom was a stronghold for pine marten even when the species was struggling in Ireland, before it got legal protection in 1970. It may be no coincidence pine marten and red squirrels both thrive here, even though invasive grey squirrels have pushed reds out elsewhere. New research suggests that greys avoid forests where pine marten are plentiful, as the marten find it easier to catch the bigger, slower greys. The red squirrel seems to have found an unwitting predatory ally.

The trail follows the edge of a field, then passes a weir and a bridge for farm vehicles. It crosses a small footbridge and follows the river down wooded lanes full with alder and willow. I picked elderberries, hazelnuts, blackberries and blackthorn sloes, and was dazzled by one hawthorn with leaves decaying from green to psychedelic yellows, oranges, purples and reds.

The trail crosses stiles along the way, many of them over electrified fences (these have rubber tubing to protect walkers). But as it progresses the river loses its character and becomes more ditch-like, hemmed in by linear banks. You pass an alder wood on your left with dark conifers beyond, and the trail continues down wooded lanes and field edges. The waymarkers direct you away from the riverbank in one small field to avoid a fording spot.

You come to a footbridge, where you can see the long straight cut of the Silver River. This would be a good spot to turn back if you are returning to Cadamstown. From here, the trail crosses the Silver River and follows more field boundaries and emerges onto a quiet road, where you could also arrange to be picked up, or leave a car.

Elderberries on the trail

Horses grazing by the Silver River

Footbridge on the Silver River

THE NORE

Dunmore Woods Loop, Durrow
(County Laois)

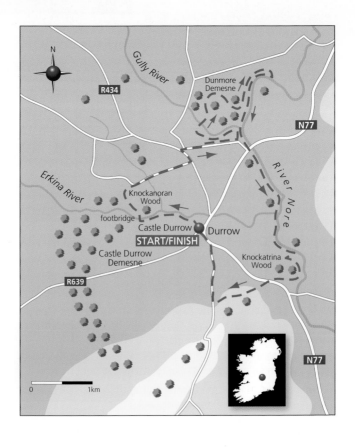

The village green at Durrow

Overview: Long walk through lush woods and farmland, with a long section on the River Nore.

Trail: You are following the green arrows of the Dunmore Woods Loop for the full walk.

Suitability: Fairly easy walking, but the trails can be rough in places, and it is a moderately long walk. Expect to encounter livestock in the fields.

Trailhead: Durrow in County Laois is on the N77 between Portlaoise and Kilkenny. It is serviced only by Slieve Bloom Coaches on its Portlaoise–Borris-in-Ossory route (www.slievebloomcoaches.ie).

Distance & time: 15km, 3½ to 5 hours.

Alternative routes: The 23km Leafy Loop is an extended version of this walk.

Maps & further info: Trail maps available to download at www.irishtrails.ie. The area is also covered by OSi *Discovery Series* Sheet 60.

This is a walk of three rivers near the Georgian village of Durrow in Laois. From the village green, follow waymarkers for the Dunmore Loop and Leafy Loop into the grounds of Castle Durrow. You will be following both trails for most of the walk.

The castle was built for local MP and landlord Colonel William Flower in the early eighteenth century. Flower developed the town alongside the estate, though there was previously a Norman village here, and the monastery of St Fintan before that.

The Erkina River

The trail turns right through a gate and down to the Erkina River. When I walked here in early autumn the river was calm and clear, coated green with duckweed and fringed with nettles and reeds. I found forget-me-nots on its verges.

From the riverside you can look back to the wide expanse of the castle. Cross the footbridge into Knockanoran Wood. This is an alluvial wood, one that floods extensively, a surprisingly rare habitat in Ireland. Coillte has dammed drains and removed non-native trees to restore the habitat and encourage damp-loving native trees like alder, willow and birch. The rare purging buckthorn occurs here too.

The trail goes left at a junction and through hazel, oak, ash, willow and birch. It then goes right down a lane thick with bracken. When you emerge onto the road, turn right and go past some houses and out along fields and woods.

After 1km you come to a busier road. Turn left, then take the first right. Continue straight and soon a waymarker on your left directs you into a beech wood and the trail goes right. There is a lot of invasive cherry laurel here, but also yews and skinny oaks with vertical branches. Exotic conifers have been removed to let

The New Bridge over the Nore at Durrow

these wood regenerate, but some oaks still reach upwards for light as in a dense forest. Durrow comes from the Irish *dair magh*, meaning 'a plain of the oaks', but there are no real oak woods left here.

The trail emerges by a car park, and when I passed, a sign informed walkers not to pick berries because the laurel had been sprayed with herbicide (having come in the back entrance, I had already gorged on blackberries).

The trail goes left, then left again. When I walked here, the light-filled patches where conifers had been felled were thick with tangles of young elder, brambles, bracken and blackthorn.

The trail swings right and crosses a footbridge over the Gully River. Here I startled a heron, which weaved through the deadfall on its way downstream. The surface of the water shook with thousands of water striders, flicking themselves forward against the current. These water-walkers are predators that pick off other invertebrates as they slide past. Trout are not fond of eating striders, so they can amass in huge gangs like the one I saw here.

Wooded path by the River Nore

The trail continues through dark mixed woods, where the trees are tightly packed. There are various side paths and junctions ahead, but keep with the green arrows. You pass cattle pasture and the former site of Dunmore House, once home to the Protestant Bishop of Ossory. The house has been demolished, but some outbuildings remain. The last family to live here, the Staples, had a strange tradition of burying their dead at midnight.

The trail goes back into the woods and turns to join the River Nore. Salmon, pike and trout all inhabit this stretch of the river. So does the endangered Nore pearl mussel, which is unique to a short stretch of water here. This species can live for more than 100 years, and is a parasite on the gills of fish early in its life cycle. However, it has not bred successfully here for decades, and it is estimated there are only 500 or so left.

There are remnants of an old bridge here, and the riverbank is rich in alder and willow. There are also ash, beech, sycamore, oak, hazel, elder and tall poplars. On narrow wooded rivers like this, lack of sunlight means there is little vegetation in the water, so fallen leaves provide most of the plant matter on which the whole ecosystem is based. Soon, the river opens to fields on the far bank, and the trail turns sandy. You cross a footbridge where the Gully River flows into the Nore, near the car park you passed earlier.

You shortly come to a busy road bridge. The trail leaves the river and joins a quiet road. Turn left, then cross the N77 (with care) to rejoin the river on its right bank through willow, birch, hazel, ash and various conifers. The trail comes to a bend where the river spills and emerges into light, and you then cross a footbridge where the Erkina joins the Nore. Both of these rivers form part of a Special Protection Area for the kingfisher.

The trail follows the river along the edge of rich, wide fields. Buoyed by the waters of the Gully and the Erkina, the Nore grows in volume. Deadfall

Near the junction of the Nore and the Erkina rivers

is less important as rivers widen because more sunlight now reaches the water to drive plant growth. And as the river widens and deepens, more and bigger fish can inhabit its waters.

The riverbank is mostly bare grass, but in the next field there is one fat oak by the water. In the next field, I passed a herd of disinterested cattle lazing by the river.

When you reach the end of the field by the woods, turn right (without crossing the fence) and continue to a gate. The chimneystacks of Knockatrina House are visible ahead. This eighteenth-century manor was another Flower family property. Knockatrina comes from the Irish *Cnoc na Traonach*, 'the hill of the corncrake', but these birds left long ago and in Ireland now breed only on the western seaboard.

The trail crosses a stile into dark stubby woods with hazel, elm, oak, ash and hawthorn, then goes into a beech plantation. When you emerge at a barrier, cross the road and turn right on the grassy verge.

There is a small monument here to the Durrow Brick Company, which thrived in the late nineteenth and early twentieth centuries. The trail goes left and climbs a forest track under more beech, then goes down a shaded farm lane.

Oak tree by the River Nore

You come to a quiet road. If you are keen to keep walking, turn left here to continue on the Leafy Loop, which will add about 8km to your walk, mostly through woods. It includes a steep climb up a hill known as the Ballagh for views over pasture and woodland. But to complete the Dunmore Woods Loop, turn right for a 1km road walk back to Durrow.

THE NORE

Nore Valley Way, Kilkenny to Bennettsbridge
(County Kilkenny)

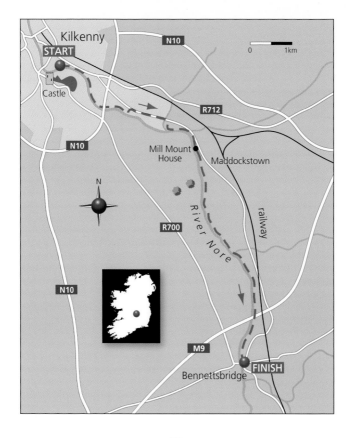

Overview: Flat walk along the banks of the River Nore through woods and farmland.

Trail: From Maudlin Street to Kilkenny ring road bridge, you are following the Lacken Walk, one of a series of trails in the Nore Linear Park, which takes in both sides of the river in the town. From the ring road bridge to Bennettsbridge, you are following the green arrows of the Nore Valley Way.

Suitability: Graded Moderate. Easy and relatively flat walking, but rough underfoot in places. Expect to encounter livestock in the fields.

Start: Maudlin Street is just off John Street, which is an extension of John's Bridge, on the opposite side of the river as the castle. Kilkenny is serviced by Bus Éireann and J. J. Kavanagh buses (www.jjkavanagh.ie), and by Irish Rail.

Finish: Bennettsbridge. The village is serviced by Bus Éireann (Athlone–Waterford service). Kilbride Coaches also services Kilkenny to Bennetsbridge.

Distance & time: 13km, 3–4 hours.

Alternative routes: The eventual plan is for the Nore Valley Way to run for 34km from Kilkenny city to Inistioge. The stretch from Bennettsbridge to Inistioge had yet to open at the time of writing, but the trail was open for the 11km walk from Thomastown to Inistioge, though a good chunk of this is on road rather than right by the river.

Services: All services in Kilkenny, shop and pub in Bennettsbridge.

Maps & further info: Trail maps available to download from www.irishtrails. ie and www.trailkilkenny.ie. The route is also covered by OSi *Discovery Series* Sheets 67 & 68.

From Kilkenny city, you can walk the Nore south through limestone flatlands. On Maudlin Street a quiet road veers off, past picnic tables by the river. Nearby is a tower house, once part of a medieval hospital that treated leprosy.

Just across the river is Kilkenny Castle, which dates from the thirteenth century. It was built for William Marshall, a Norman settler who married Strongbow's daughter. The castle was extended and rebuilt over the centuries, but three of the original towers survive.

Marshall drove the development of the town too, though *Cill Cheannaigh* had been an important monastic site for centuries before. James Butler, the third Earl of Ormond, bought the castle in 1319. It remained in his family until the twentieth century, when a local restoration committee bought it for £50.

Climb the steps at the end of this cul-de-sac, but halfway up turn right down the lane. You pass the ruins of the Lacken corn mill, which dates from the 1770s, and come to the riverside. The river was smooth and shallow when I walked here in early September, and the water was a still clear green, moving imperceptibly south. The day was hot and hazy, and I watched a banded demoiselle damselfly flit along the riverbank.

The trail follows a boardwalk along the wooded riverbank and then goes under the bridge of the ring road. Here you will see the first green 'Trail Kilkenny' waymarker, which you will be following all the way to Bennettsbridge. You go by rough pasture and woodland, and through old stone walls, and rejoin the Nore by dark woods.

Soon the trail leaves the river, climbs up to the Sion Road and turns right. Take great care here: the footpath eventually disappears, and there are dangerous corners along the road. There are arrows on poles to let you know you are on the right track. On the right, you pass a road that leads down to Brett's Saw Mills, a working mill with a circular saw powered

The Lacken Walk

by a waterwheel. Unsurprisingly, the mill manufactures hurleys, among other items.

After 1km on the road, a waymarker on your right directs you over a stile into a field. Follow the left edge of the field down to the quickening river, under hedgerows of beech, ash, blackthorn and hawthorn. At the riverbank the trail goes left through more pasture, under willow and ash. Then you cross a footbridge into woodland, and a bit further on, pass the garden of a house.

I rested on a grassy verge, where the river spilled over a small weir and turned from peat brown to foam white. I scanned the water intently, hoping to see an otter or maybe a kingfisher. But nothing moved. Water striders slid over the river surface, and while I sometimes heard fish jumping, I saw none. The air was thick with the smells of autumn: leaves decaying, fruit ripening, fungus emerging.

On the Nore Valley Way

The trail passes through the ruins of a marble sawmill before emerging to rough pasture under Mill Mount House. The house was built in the late eighteenth century for

Weir on the Nore

William Colles, who opened the marble quarries nearby, and invented machinery for sawing, boring and polishing the rock. Colles was the first person to power these processes with water. Under the house, the ruins of another mill are lost in the overgrowth.

The land here is an order-less and glorious patchwork of woodland, scrub, meadow and pasture. The big pink flowers of Himalayan balsam, an invasive species, were out all along the verge of the river when I went by. But I also found flowering poppies, forget-me-nots and charlock.

The trail goes back into the woods, through the stark ruins of vast overgrown mills. The buildings here at Maddockstown date from between the sixteenth and nineteenth centuries, and served different milling functions, but marble milling was the main activity. Could modern industrial estates, if consumed by nature, ever be this enchanting?

The trail runs through woods and under quarried walls of carboniferous limestone. This is the marble for which Kilkenny is known and which was milled nearby, but although it is slick and black, it is not true marble. Ash and beech trees emanate from the rock, and there are big oaks along here too.

After more woodland the trail follows the edge of a field by the river. Most leaves were still green when I walked here, although I found one hedgerow birch that had decayed into a shocking array of neon reds, purples, yellows and oranges. Up ahead the river splits around an island of willow.

Mill Mount House above the River Nore

Ash and willow on the river

The trail crosses another field and goes through more wooded lanes at the edge of fields. There are limestone quarries on both sides of the Nore here, but the trees shield you.

Eventually the sound of traffic looms ahead, and you arrive under a motorway bridge. Stand under the bridge and look up: it is difficult not to be impressed by this precise, symmetrical, vast work of engineering.

The trail crosses more fields and soon you arrive, past oaks and rowan, at Bennettsbridge. This village once sat on the main road south from Leinster, when travellers forded the river. The bridge was built in 1783. Downstream on the far bank is a tall old mill, now a pottery, an elegant punctuation mark to this walk.

Willow overhanging the River Nore beside a Nore Valley Way marker

The Barrow Way

Introduction to the Barrow Way

The Barrow Way runs for 114km through Kildare, Laois and Carlow. From Robertstown in County Kildare, it follows the Barrow Line of the Grand Canal to Athy. It then follows the River Barrow for 66km south to St Mullin's, County Carlow. Here the river becomes tidal. I have broken the route into five day-walks. You may wish to undertake longer or shorter stages depending on your preferred pace. I walked the route with two friends during the summer and early autumn of 2014. The landscape becomes more dramatic the further south you go. At the time of writing there were controversial plans to pave the Barrow Way with 'clean stone and compacted quarry dust' to make it more suitable for cyclists. My description reflects the state of the towpaths as they were when I walked the trail.

COUNTY KILDARE

Robertstown to Rathangan to Monasterevin
(County Kildare)

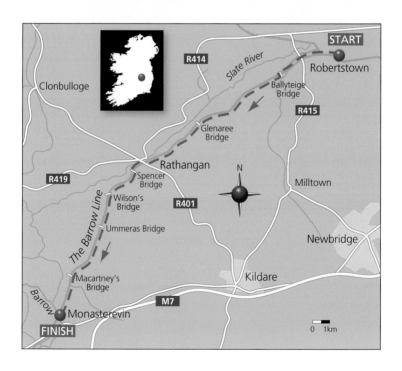

On the towpath south of Rathangan

Overview: Canalside walk, mostly on grassy towpaths, through farmland, forestry and scrub.

Trail: You are following the Barrow Way. When I walked the trail, from Rathangan Bridge the official route went along the left-hand bank of the canal between this bridge and Spencer Bridge at the other end of the town. But the left bank follows a road, which has no footpath at the approach to Spencer Bridge so I recommend crossing the canal, on the footbridge just after Rathangan Bridge, and following the right bank to Spencer Bridge, where you cross back to the left-hand side.

Suitability: Flat walk on easy terrain, but the full route is a long day.

Trailheads: Robertstown, County Kildare, is located between Prosperous, Allenwood and Kilmeague in the north of the county. It is serviced by Bus Éireann (Dublin–Newbridge route).

Rathangan is at the junction of the R401, R414 and R419 in northwest County Kildare. The town is serviced by Bus Éireann (Dublin to Kildare route).

Monasterevin, County Kildare, is on the R445 between Kildare town and Portlaoise. Take exit 14 off the M7 Dublin–Limerick motorway. The town is serviced by Irish Rail and Dublin Coach (www.dublincoach.ie).

Distance & time: Robertstown to Rathangan is 14km, 3½ to 4½ hours. Rathangan to Monasterevin is 10.5km, 2½ to 3½ hours.

Services: Shops and pubs at Robertstown; supermarket, shops, pubs, food at Rathangan. All services plus limited accommodation at Monasterevin.

Map & further info: Trail maps from www.irishtrails.ie. Also the *Guide to the Grand Canal of Ireland* (Inland Waterways Association of Ireland). Online version at www.iwai.ie. OSi *Discovery Series* Sheets 49 and 55.

Robertsown to Rathangan

Near the Milltown branch of the Grand Canal

Early in its construction, the directors of the Grand Canal chose to link the waterway with the River Barrow and work began on the Barrow Line of the Grand Canal in 1783.

At Robertstown, the first Barrow Way sign directs you across Binn's Bridge and along a quiet road on the right bank of the canal. The canal curves to the nineteenth lock, where there is a cottage with a giant keyhole in its front door. Cross Fenton Bridge here, by Lowtown marina, and go left. Follow the towpath along this canal, known as the Old Barrow Line. There is a newer line just parallel to the north. You then join a quiet road.

Eyebright flowered on the grassy verge when I passed here, and there was great willowherb, bindweed and common reed – typical canalside species – in the fringe between land and water. Cross the road by Littletown Bridge, staying on the right bank. Look for the Hill of Allen, the legendary home of Fionn Mac Cumhaill, way off to the left. The tower on its summit is a nineteenth-century folly.

Soon the Milltown branch (see Route 4) of the canal veers off under a bridge on the far bank. Strangely, an inscription on one side of this bridge reads '1788 Huband Bridge', while the other side says '1799 Greene Bridge'. Huband was an early director of the Grand Canal Company, while Greene was company secretary.

The Milltown Feeder is the Grand Canal's principal water supply, drawing on Pollardstown Fen, a spring-fed wetland. Cross Skew Bridge, where the new and old Barrow Lines meet beyond the old nineteenth lock, and turn left. You are now at the western end of the summit level, the 9km 'pound' – a stretch of canal between two locks – that forms the highest section of the Grand Canal, 82m above sea level.

Just before Ballyteige Castle, cross the bridge to the left bank. Silken Thomas is said to have

Cattle grazing by the canal near Rathangan

Macartney's Bridge and the twenty-fourth lock on the Barrow Line

sheltered here during his rebellion against King Henry VIII, after hearing false rumours that his father, Gerald Fitz-gerald, the ninth Earl of Kildare, had been executed in the Tower of London.

The towpath passes two locks, and when I walked here the common reeds, with their purple flowers out, were so tall I couldn't see the water. I also found St John's wort and wild marjoram flowering on the towpath. There is conifer forestry beyond fields on the far bank, and beyond that again, invisible from here, the vast Bog of Allen.

The original canal suffered from sinking across Ballyteige Bog, so this channel was built instead. No trace of the old line remains. After you pass the last house on the left, the Griffith Aqueduct brings you over a tributary of the Slate River. Scrub, bog and forestry interweave here, and on the far bank the fields become expansive and prairie-like.

You emerge onto a quiet road by a stone-clad house, where you might see a strange square boat moored. Local farmers, with fields on both sides, apparently use these to pole across the canal. Follow the quiet road as hedgerows enclose the waterway. Ten kilometres from Robertstown, you arrive at Glenaree lock and bridge. There is an elegant Georgian farmhouse just off to the left. Past here, dark forestry closes in and the towpath grows remote again. When I walked here in late August, the red berries of hawthorn and guelder rose coloured the hedgerows.

After the forestry on your left there is open scrub. Farmers and ecologists often deride scrub, for different reasons, but to me this is nature at its best: unruly and chaotic. Soon you see Rathangan Bridge ahead, 14km from Robertstown. There are ruined stone warehouses just before the bridge, and you can still see the rath (or ring fort) for which the town is named by going right at the bridge and going up Main Street. Rathangan's Georgian townhouses were built at the same time as the canal.

Rathangan to Monasterevin

To continue along the canal, cross the footbridge just beyond the road bridge, and take the footpath on the right bank of the canal to Spencer Bridge and the twenty-third lock. Cross back to the left bank here. This bridge was named after local landowner James Spencer, who sold land for the construction of the canal. He was later piked to death by insurgents on the stairs of his home during the 1798 Rebellion. There is an old harbour just beyond the bridge.

Past Rathangan the canal becomes a world entirely of its own, far from roads and houses. When it bends and trees overhang, it feels at its wildest and most river-like. My footfall sent a coot flapping across the channel, deep into reeds, and under Wilson's Bridge the water was thick with spaghetti-like milfoils. Further on, the towpath was dotted with the lilac of field scabious, and the hedgerows were full of alder. One of my walking buddies found two froglets, fingernail-sized, clinging tight to grass blades.

The canal goes through forestry again. You then come to a quiet road, pass a thatched cottage and follow the towpath to Ummeras Bridge, 5km beyond Rathangan. Elderberries were out in the hedgerows here, ripening from green to purple, and across the water cattle grazed narrow pasture. Even when it flows near big farms, the land beside the canal tends to be wonderfully marginal: hedgerows, scrub, ditches and wetlands.

The canal arrives at the twenty-fourth lock and Macartney's Bridge. There is a thatched cottage hidden in the foliage on the far bank. Cross the road and continue on the left bank of the canal. Soon the vast and derelict Ballykelly Mill rises on your left. The mill dates from 1801, and there are now plans to turn it into a distillery. The surface of the canal was dotted with flowering water lilies here, while reeds and willow grew tall along its fringe.

The houses of Monasterevin soon come into view. Follow the towpath under Shepherd's Brook Bridge and along a road into the town. You go under a rail bridge and arrive at the harbour.

You can turn left at the harbour and follow Drogheda Street into the town centre. Monasterevin has some fine Georgian architecture, and was a favourite getaway of the poet Gerard Manley Hopkins. The town is said to derive its name from a monastery founded here by St Evin. It is believed this monastery was on the site now occupied by Moore Abbey, an eighteenth-century Gothic mansion once occupied by the renowned tenor Count John McCormack.

The Grand Canal near Monasterevin

THE BARROW WAY

Monasterevin to Vicarstown to Athy
(Counties Kildare & Laois)

Overview: Flat walk mostly on mostly grassy canal towpaths through rural Kildare and Laois.

Trail: You are following the Barrow Way.

Suitability: Flat walking along easy surfaces but the full route is a very long day.

Trailheads: Monasterevin, County Kildare is on the R445 between Kildare town and Portlaoise. Take exit 14 off the M7 Dublin–Limerick motorway. The town is serviced by Irish Rail and Dublin Coach (www.dublincoach.ie).

Vicarstown is on the R427 in County Laois, 6km northeast of Stradbally. It has no public transport.

Athy is on the N78 in south county Kildare. It is well serviced by Bus Éireann and J. J. Kavanagh buses (www.jjkavanagh.ie), and by Irish Rail.

Distance & time: Monasterevin to Vicarstown, 12km, 3 to 4 hours. Vicarstown to Athy, 10.5km, 2½ to 3½ hours.

Services: Pubs, food, shops, limited accommodation in Monasterevin and Athy; pub (open in the evenings) and self-catering accommodation at Vicarstown. There is a freshwater tap at Vicarstown in the corner of the yard in front of Barrowline Cruisers.

Map & further info: Download trail maps from www.irishtrails.ie. Also the *Guide to the Grand Canal of Ireland* (Inland Waterways Association of Ireland). Online version at www.iwai.ie. OSi *Discovery Series* Sheet 55.

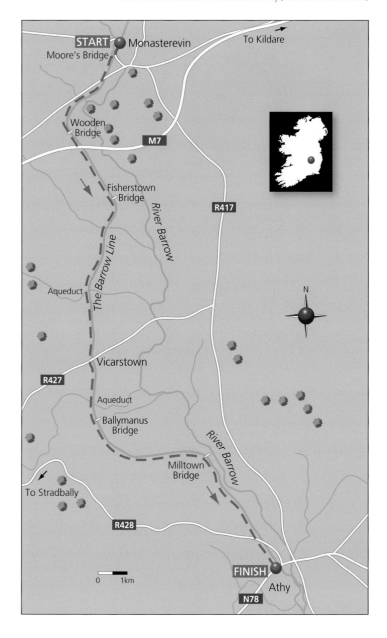

Barges moored at Vicarstown

Monasterevin to Vicarstown

The Barrow Line of the Grand Canal reached Monasterevin in 1785. The original plan was for it to join the River Barrow here. There must, however, have been some concern about how navigable the river was, because the canal continues to Athy. More than 4,000 men worked on the Barrow Line during its construction. Inaccurate surveys led to errors in its construction and it ultimately cost a colossal £500,000 rather than the projected £98,000.

Facing the harbour in Monasterevin, turn left and follow the canal along the road, then onto a grassy path as it swings right. Cross the road by the lifting bridge. Continue on the left bank, and over the 1820s aqueduct where the canal crosses the River Barrow. During freezing winters, water seeping through the masonry of the aqueduct can form dramatic icicles under its arches.

The derelict Mountmellick Branch of the canal splits off from the far bank. This was meant to reach the Castlecomer coalfields 50km away in Kilkenny, but only got as far as Mountmellick, less than half the way. At the twenty-fifth lock, turn right to follow the waymarker over Moore's Bridge, by a small harbour. Follow the gravel track out to a road, then take the towpath under the road bridge. The towpath just beyond the bridge was overgrown when I passed.

You briefly emerge onto a quiet road and then the canal becomes wooded and enclosed. You can hear cars in the distance, but this heightens the sense of isolation: being aware of the world beyond only makes the waterway feel more secret. The fringes of the canal were overgrown with reeds and rushes when I walked here in late summer, and I found pink-flowering woundwort on the towpath.

We made camp here under willows at the end of our first day on the Barrow Way. The sun dropped behind the hedgerows, the sky faded to indigo, then the canal turned the same colour. The day had been dull and grey, but at dawn the next morning the sun rose and blasted everything with amber light.

You pass a farmstead and come to a quiet road. Carry on along the canal, under the motorway and through a barrier past cattle sheds. When I passed here, the hazel-rich hedgerows were heavy with fresh nuts. You reach Fisherstown Bridge, where there is a thatched pub 400m up the road to your right.

Walking near Fisherstown Bridge

Sunshine near Vicarstown

Here the canal flows through the valley of the Barrow; the river is parallel to the east. There is a quiet boreen on the far bank here too, lined with rustic farmhouses. It was early morning when I walked here and, as the sun rose, dragonflies, butterflies and bees emerged. On the embankment, a gang of peacock butterflies sucked nectar from a buddleia bush.

The towpath passes under Courtwood Bridge and follows wide cattle fields. As you continue south along the Barrow Way, the rough fields and forestry around the bogs of northern Kildare turn into more productive farmscapes. 'People actually make money from farming down here,' was how one of my walking buddies, a farmer from Mayo, put it.

Soon the Grattan Aqueduct carries you and the canal over the Glasha River through soft woods. Henry Grattan, the nineteenth-century MP who opposed the Act of Union, had a home nearby. The towpath emerges at Vicarstown, where barges and cruisers are moored. There is one pub here, which opens in the evenings.

Vicarstown to Athy

Past the bridge at Vicarstown, there is a stone bench commissioned by the Laois Patrick Kavanagh Appreciation Society, inscribed with the poet's words: 'And Look! A barge comes bringing from Athy and other far flung towns mythologies.'

There is a quiet road on the far bank from here to Athy. The towpath crosses the Camac Aqueduct over the wooded River Stradbally. It then passes under Ballymanus Bridge, and by a hotchpotch of woodland and forestry on the far bank. You might notice a strong smell here; there is a mink farm to your right. The willowherb and bindweed were both flowering when I walked here, as were the water-lilies on the still surface of the canal.

After the woods on the far bank recede, the canal passes rich pasture under hedgerows with alder, willow and elder. You will see more houses as Athy nears. To the north is Castle Rheban, which dates from the fifteenth century. During construction of the farmhouse in the early twentieth century, workers found a skeleton hand clutching fifteenth-century coins. The castle guarded a ford on the River Barrow, and was the site of an ancient town.

The canal curves and goes under Milltown Bridge. If you climb up to the bridge, you can see Bert House, a showy Georgian mansion built for Captain William Burgh, Comptroller and Accountant General for Ireland. The River Barrow is just below the house.

Past Milltown Bridge the towpath was deeply overgrown when I passed. You can also follow the road here and rejoin the towpath through a gate up ahead. The towpath goes past Cardington Bridge, under Lennon's Bridge and follows an avenue of tall trees into Athy. This town was built by a ford on the Barrow. Its name is derived from *Athe-Ae*, meaning the ford of Ae. Legend says Ae was a warrior who was killed here in a second-century battle between the armies of Leinster and Munster. Athy was later developed by Norman settlers, and endured frequent attacks from the native Irish.

Wide skies near Milltown Bridge

You pass old stone warehouses and arrive at Augustus Bridge, near new and old industrial buildings. Turn left here for the town centre. The Grand Canal reached Athy in 1791. In the past, to avoid tolls, boats sometimes used the river rather than the canal north of here. The town has a heritage centre with a permanent exhibition on the Antarctic explorer Ernest Shackleton, who was born nearby.

White's Castle, on the River Barrow in the town centre, was built in 1417 to guard the river. The castle was sold in 2005 for €1.3 million, but in 2012 it was sold again for just €195,000. Beside the bridge, we watched an otter slink along an embankment under the castle, unseen by the bustling town.

THE BARROW WAY

Athy to Maganey to Carlow
(Counties Kildare & Carlow)

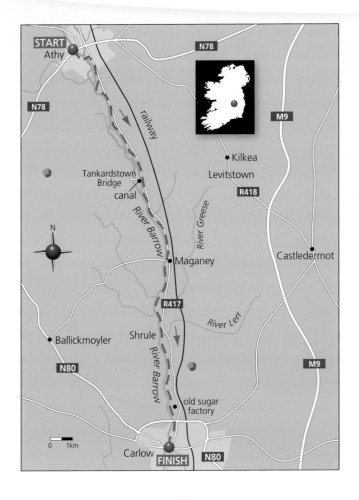

Overview: Flat walk along the towpath of the winding River Barrow and its side canals through rural Kildare and Carlow.

Trail: You are following the Barrow Way.

Suitability: Flat walking, mostly on grassy surfaces, but a long enough day.

Trailheads: Athy, County Kildare, is on the N78 in south county Kildare. It is well serviced by Bus Éireann and J. J. Kavanagh buses, and by Irish Rail.

Maganey is on the R417 between Carlow Town and Athy. It has no public transport.

Finish: Carlow Town is on the N80 and just off the M9. It is well serviced by Bus Éireann and J. J. Kavanagh (www.jjkavanagh.ie) buses, and by Irish Rail.

Distance & time: Athy to Maganey is 10.5km, 2½ to 3½ hours. Maganey to Carlow is 8.5km, 2 to 3 hours.

Services: Shops, supermarkets, pubs, accommodation in Athy and Carlow. Shop at Maganey.

Map & further info: Trail maps from www.irishtrails.ie. Also the *Guide to the Barrow Navigation* (the Inland Waterways Association of Ireland). Online version at www.iwai.ie. OSi *Discovery Series* Sheets 55 and 61.

Maganey Bridge

Athy to Maganey

In Athy, the Barrow Way joins the river for which it is named. From Augustus Bridge on the canal, follow the right bank south past the Tegral factory to the twenty-eighth lock. Cross the footbridge on the lock, then turn right and cross the old horse bridge, where the river and canal meet.

The wooded River Barrow south of Athy

Turn right and follow the river under a rail bridge along the wooded towpath on the left bank. This derelict rail line was built to serve the coalfields of Castlecomer, County Kilkenny.

The trail leaves the river by a weir and joins a side canal. Weirs were built on the river to provide a good head of water for the side canals, enabling boats to navigate around any hazards on the river. There are almost 18km of canal along the River Barrow.

The towpath brings you to Ardreigh Lock and drawbridge. The bridge once served a four-storey flourmill on Lord's Island, to your right. The mill's owner was found shot dead in odd circumstances in 1923. His death was ruled an accident, but a servant reported hearing strange movements in the house that day.

The towpath rejoins the river. Now the Barrow forms the boundary between Kildare on this side and Laois on the opposite. The river curves through farmland before becoming more wooded. The sun came out as I walked here after showers, past hedgerows with birch, willow and Scots pine, and the river's edge was thick with willowherb, bindweed and nettles. Compared to the canal, the wide arcs of the river were exhilarating.

You come to a weir where the towpath joins another side channel. This is the Levitstown Cut, the longest canal on the

Stone footbridge on the Levitstown Cut

The derelict seven-storey mill at Levitstown

Barrow. It feels like a forgotten waterway, enclosed by lush foliage and little navigated. Two stone footbridges provide access to the island of scrub and pasture on your right.

Along here, I noticed only my third oak since starting the Barrow Way in Robertstown. I also found an odd mushroom, the red-cracked bolete, sprouting from the towpath.

You come to Tankardstown Bridge, and then the towering old mill and lock at Levitstown. Malt was once prepared here and transported by barge to Guinness in Dublin, but the mill was ruined by a fire in 1942. Pass the lock and follow the towpath back along the river.

The wooded Barrow looks out to wide fields and eventually splits in two around a slim island, a fragment of wilderness too small to cultivate. I found poppies growing from the gravel towpath before the seven-arched Maganey Bridge, and saw a kingfisher flicker across the river, metallic blue. This would seem to be a good place to see these birds, as Michael Fewer also reported seeing them here in his 1996 book, *The Waymarked Trails of Ireland*.

At Maganey Bridge in 1642, the Earl of Ormond's army defeated 8,000 troops from the Confederacy of Irish Catholics, an alliance of native chieftains and old English settlers. At the end our second day on the Barrow Way, we made camp here in the late evening.

Maganey to Carlow

Carry on south under Maganey Bridge. I walked here in the early morning and watched a cormorant fly inelegantly upstream. The Barrow was dark and smooth, flowing slowly. A kingfisher ducked into roots on the riverbank, and along the towpath morning anglers were out fishing for trout.

Soon you come to Maganey Lock on another side cut. The lock cottage bears an inscription to the writer Eugene Waters, better known as Eoghan Ó Tuairisc, who lived here. As you walk south, the hedgerows open up to reveal the fields around you, then close in again. The woods are only a few trees deep, but in late summer they were thick and full, obscuring the world beyond.

The towpath crosses a footbridge where the River Greese flows into the Barrow and another over the River Lerr. The sixteenth-century Shrule Castle is across the river in the trees opposite the latter river. The far bank becomes more deeply wooded as you pass the grounds of Knockbeg College. The towpath goes down a wooded lane with willow, ash, horse-chestnut, hawthorn and alder.

After another weir, the towpath follows a canal to Bestfield Lock, which folklore says is haunted.

You rejoin the wide river as it nears Carlow town. The towpath passes the site of the former sugar factory and the town starts to reveal itself before you. After going under a road bridge you pass an ancient cemetery known as the Graves. Nearby is a plot where bodies were dumped during the cholera epidemic in 1849. St Mary's Church of Ireland is straight ahead, and off to the left is the Catholic cathedral.

You join a footpath along the river, and carry on past the rowing club and up to the Graiguecullen (or Wellington) Bridge. Downstream of here the Barrow navigation struggled due to low water in summer, but commercial trade boats still came as far down as Carlow until they were withdrawn in 1959.

THE BARROW WAY

Carlow to Leighlinbridge to Goresbridge

(County Carlow)

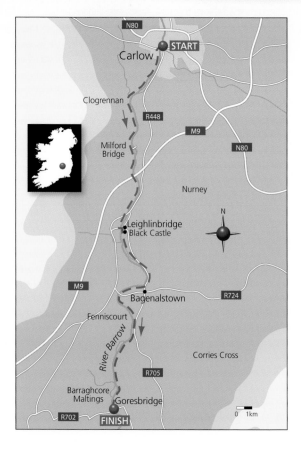

Near Clogrennan on the Barrow

Overview: Flat towpath walk along the River Barrow and its side canals, meandering through farmland, woodland and small towns.

Trail: You are following the Barrow Way

Suitability: Flat and easy walking but the full route is a long, strenuous day.

Trailheads: Carlow town is on the N80 and just off the M9. It is well serviced by Bus Éireann and J. J. Kavanagh (www.jjkavanagh.ie) buses, and by Irish Rail.

Leighlinbridge is in west County Carlow, just off the R448 and R705. It is also just off exit 6 on the M9. It is serviced by Bus Éireann and J. J. Kavanagh.

Finish: Goresbridge, County Kilkenny, is on the R702 between Gowran, County Kilkenny and Borris, County Carlow. It is 13.5km east of Kilkenny city. It is serviced by Kilbride Coaches from Kilkenny.

Distance & time: Carlow to Leighlinbridge is 11km, 2½ to 3½ hours. Leighlinbridge to Goresbridge is 14.5 km, 3½ to 5 hours.

Services: Shops, pubs and accommodation in Carlow, Leighlinbridge and Bagenalstown; shop and pubs in Goresbridge.

Map & further info: Trail maps from www.irishtrails.ie. Also the *Guide to the Barrow Navigation* (the Inland Waterways Association of Ireland). Online version at www.iwai.ie. OSi *Discovery Series* Sheets 61 and 68.

Carlow to Leighlinbridge

Having spent two and a half days walking the Barrow Way from Robertstown to Carlow in August, blisters and rain halted our plans to complete the trail, so we came back a few weeks later.

Heading south from Carlow town, the Barrow Way crosses the Graiguecullen Bridge from the left to the right bank of the river. Look across the river and you can see Carlow Castle. Like Kilkenny Castle, this

was built by the Norman settler William Marshall, who married Strongbow's daughter. But it was destroyed in the nineteenth century during a botched attempt to use explosives to refurbish it into an insane asylum.

Soon you pass a weir and a side cut that leads down to Carlow Lock; then you come back to the river, its banks rich in willow and reeds. The river

Walking towards Millford

traces the edges of the town and emerges into open countryside. You then come to Clogrennan Weir, the only natural weir on the Barrow. The towpath follows a long side canal down to the lock, past a narrow island of mid-river willow. In early autumn, the hedgerows here were dark with ripe blackberries, sloes and elderberries.

The towpath goes through the yard of a privately owned lock house. You rejoin the river past the lock and cross a footbridge where the Fushoge River flows into the Barrow. Soon you pass the ruins of Clogrennan Castle, which was built in the fifteenth century. It later became a gate lodge for nearby Clogrennan House, but that too is now ruined. Up ahead is the early nineteenth-century Cloydagh Church.

Past here the roads recede and the river quietens. When I walked here, the dead-still water reflected yellowing willows that were illuminated by the afternoon sun high above Clogrennan Hill to the west.

Soon the river divides into a labyrinth of channels and islands, and a side canal leads down to Milford Lock,

The approach to Millford Lock

while the river flows onwards under Milford Bridge, which was built in the 1760s.

The ruined monolithic facade of Milford Mills rises across the bridge. Three large grain mills were built here in the 1790s, but a huge fire ripped through the complex in 1862. The waterwheel came to life again in the 1890s, driving a dynamo to provide electricity and public lighting to Carlow town. With quarries and coalmines nearby, this was once a busy port. But today the river is quiet.

The largest building at the mills later became a tannery, employing ninety people, but another fire destroyed this in 1965. However, hydropower is still produced here and exported to the national grid.

On the side canal the trees close over and the greens of the foliage, towpath and canal all merge into one. You pass under sycamore, elder, oak, ash, holly and elm, and beyond the lifting bridge tall woods rise on the far bank of the river. Soon the Barrow divides around Aughnabinnia Island, and you go under the M9 motorway.

The river divides around more islands, wonderfully named the Orchard Islands. The further I walked down the Barrow, the more fascinated I became with these river islands, fragments of wilderness beyond my reach.

You come past hedgerows full with willow and alder to the weir and lock at Rathvinden. When I went by here there was a rusted barge on the water, with willow sprouting right from its hull.

The towpath goes under the Cardinal Moran Bridge and you can soon see Leighlinbridge ahead (pronounced 'Locklenbridge'). The river splits around more willow islands before coming to the village. I have read in various places that at least part of the bridge here dates from 1320, but can find no authoritative source for this.

The Barrow Way switches from the right to left bank of the river here. On the towpath is a sign recounting the fascinating life of the famous physicist and mountaineer John Tyndall, who was born here and became a professor at London's prestigious Royal Institution.

Walking south from Leighlinbridge along the Barrow Way

Tyndall would apparently work out geometry problems while walking to school on the towpath with his teacher. He was also part of the first team to climb the Weisshorn in the Alps. Giving a speech at his retirement dinner, Tyndall said: 'The hardest climb, by far, that I have accomplished, was that from the banks of the Barrow to the banks of the Thames.' (His mountaineering exploits are detailed in one chapter of Frank Nugent's book, *In Search of Peaks, Passes & Glaciers.*)

Leighlinbridge to Goresbridge

Leaving Leighlinbridge on the left bank you pass the Black Castle, which dates from the fourteenth century. The local chieftain Rory Óg O'More captured the tower from Sir Peter Carew in 1577, destroying it in the process. Rory Óg rebuilt it, only for Cromwell's armies to attack it again later.

Soon you pass a weir, around which the river sprawls like a delta, and the towpath enters the shaded Rathelin Cut, which is rich with ash and willow, hawthorn and alder, hazel and holly. Stone bridges span the still water to the island of rough grazing on your right. Before rejoining the river, the towpath crosses a stone bridge, part of an old dry dock and workshops.

When I passed in autumn, the proprietors of the house here had left out fresh apples for walkers. We took one, and stole from their plum tree too, but left a generous tip in the jar they provided. Soon you can see the outdoor swimming pool of Bagenalstown, or Muine Bheag, ahead on the towpath. There are normally lifeguards on the river here in summer for swimmers. You pass a chain of weirs and islands and arrive at the town.

Bagenalstown was named for the local landowner Walter Bagenal. I have read in a few places that Bagenal wanted to create an Irish version of Versailles here, only to be thwarted when an important coach road was

Walking into Bagenalstown

diverted elsewhere. But evidence for this story seems slim. The town was given its Irish name, after a local townland, in the 1930s. But locals still call it Bagenalstown.

You will pass elegant old mill buildings on the way into the town, and the way out. Leaving Bagenalstown, the Barrow curves around the fringes of the town rather than heading straight south, and it takes a while to leave the industrial buildings on its edges behind. The willow-rich towpath passes under the Royal Oak road bridge, then an elegant limestone rail viaduct. The whole Barrow towpath is a good place to see butterflies in the warmer months: common blues, silver-washed and dark green fritillaries,

Morning mist on the Barrow

brimstones, red admirals and orange tips.

Having started from Carlow in the afternoon, we arrived at the weir and lock at Fenniscourt as the sun sank. At dusk the sky turned a blend of purple, white, orange and red, while not being singly any one of these colours, and swallows picked off midges in the blue haze over the water.

You rejoin the river through soft pasture, and the Barrow valley, away from roads, grows quiet. Further on, the towpath crosses a bridge by an old harbour, and you come to a long weir – the oldest on the navigation – before the cut down to Slyguff Lock. We made camp by the lock at dusk under beech trees, and the next morning we set out in the pale dawn.

You come to Ballyellen Weir, where the navigation goes down another side cut. Across the river here are the ruins of Barraghcore Maltings, a six-storey Gothic mill built around 1800. It was first used as a flourmill, then for malting barley.

Walking down this canal in the early morning, the ghostly Ballyellen Lime Works rose from

Upper Ballyellen Lock

the pale mist. We passed Upper Ballyellen Lock and made our way into Goresbridge as the cool sun rose. The vast white building that rises on the opposite bank here is an animal-feed factory.

Goresbridge is on the far bank (in County Kilkenny), but take care as there is no footpath on the eighteenth-century bridge, and the steps up to it are fairly primitive. There is an old stone warehouse on the river here. Goresbridge was once a busy harbour, with lots of mills nearby and a brewery too. During the 1798 Rebellion, Wexford insurgents defeated Crown forces here, capturing more than a dozen soldiers.

THE BARROW WAY

Goresbridge to Graiguenamanagh to St Mullin's
(County Carlow)

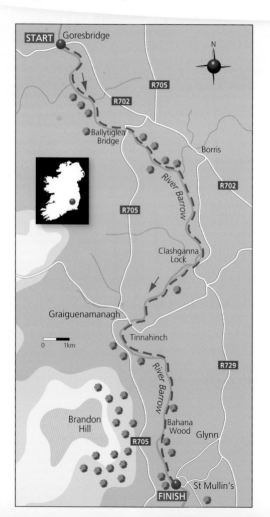

Overview: Stunning towpath walk along the River Barrow and its side canals through a deep wooded valley.

Trail: You are following the Barrow Way.

Suitability: Flat and easy walking but a long day.

Trailheads: Goresbridge, County Kilkenny, is on the R702 between Gowran, County Kilkenny and Borris, County Carlow. It is 13.5km east of Kilkenny city. Kilbride Coaches serves Goresbridge from Kilkenny city.

Graiguenamanagh is in east County Kilkenny on the R703, 17km east of Thomastown and 10km south of Borris. It is also serviced by Kilbride Coaches.

Finish: St Mullin's is rather out of the way in south County Carlow, being deep in the Barrow valley, about 2.2km southwest of the small village of Glynn, which is on the R729. There is no public transport to St Mullin's.

Distance & time: Goresbridge to Graiguenamanagh is 14.5km, 3½ to 5 hours. Graiguenamanagh to St Mullin's is 8km, 2 to 2½ hours.

Services: Shop and pubs at Goresbridge; shop, pubs and accommodation at Graiguenamanagh; café at St Mullin's.

Map & further info: Trail maps from www.irishtrails.ie. Also the *Guide to the Barrow Navigation* (the Inland Waterways Association of Ireland). Online version at www.iwai.ie. OSi *Discovery Series* Sheet 68.

The forested Barrow south of Goresbridge

f you only walk one stretch of the Barrow Way, make it this one. From Goresbridge south, the valley turns into a dramatic gorge as steep wooded hills slope to the twisting river.

Follow the Barrow Way south on the left bank from Goresbridge. The towpath passes a weir and follows a short side canal under alder, sycamore ash, hazel and beech. After Lower Ballyellen Lock, look for Barrowmount House on the far bank, the former home of the Gore family for who the village is named. The Gores came from Hertfordshire around 1700, having been granted land seized from the native Irish. There is a collapsed megalithic tomb, dating from 2000 BC, near the house.

The river turns wilder and quieter as tall spruces and pines lean over the channel. When I walked here, cattle sheltered under scrubby willow on the far bank and a heron fished from a white rock mid-river. This is a good stretch of the river to look for otters and the muddy slides they create when entering the water. Long-eared owls inhabit the woods here too.

There is a chain of weirs and woody islands before Ballytiglea Lock, and past the lock the towpath goes under the road bridge of the same name, which is a nesting place for swifts. The neat village of Borris, known for its granite buildings, is a 2.5km road walk from here.

Now the woods along the river start to deepen and thicken, and the towpath follows a side cut down to Borris Lock as the trees of Borris Demesne rise on your left.

This estate was home to the legendary Arthur MacMurrough Kavanagh, and his descendants still live here. Born without arms or legs, Arthur nonetheless became skilled at some adventurous pursuits, including sailing, horse-riding, hunting, fishing and archery, and travelled widely throughout Asia.

He was known for having a stuffed bear at his side when tenants visited, and as an MP he would sail a schooner down the Barrow, across the Irish Sea and up the Thames to Westminster. The Borris estate has impressive woods, including old oaks and huge limes and poplars.

In spring and summer, listen here for the songs of the willow warbler, the blackcap and the chiffchaff, which all migrate from the Mediterranean or Africa. Little egrets, small white herons more usually seen by the sea, also inhabit this stretch of the river.

Past Borris Lock you emerge back onto the wide river, which is hemmed in by sloping forested banks. Far from roads, the valley is silent.

Walking towards Graiguenamanagh

I stopped here to watch the water: in some parts it was dark and smooth, in others shimmering white. I tried to work out what combination of wind, water and light creates these shapeless glistening patterns on a river's surface, but obviously failed.

Mature woods along the Barrow Way

The towpath crosses a bridge where the Mountain River flows into the Barrow. You come to Ballingrane Lock, with a derelict lock cottage nearby. A little further on is Clashganna Lock, where there is an archipelago of islands on the river. There is a bathing area just upstream of the lock that is patrolled by a lifeguard in summer. 'If anyone likes wild swimming, the Barrow is the place to be,' local naturalist Mary White tells me. 'The river is mysterious, it's ever-changing. The light is always different, and the quality of the water.'

Cattle taking shade under riverside willows

Now the Barrow flows through a deep valley, with steep forested walls. As the Barrow winds towards Graiguenamanagh (known locally as Graigue), tall conifers rise from its banks, while scraps of pasture and scrub appear too.

You pass Ballykeenan Lock. As you near the village, you can see the boardwalk of Silair Wood across the river, and Brandon Hill rises dead ahead. There are rock faces here wooded with oak, beech, willow, birch, Scots pine and ash.

When you come to the bridge, you are in Tinnahinch, County Carlow. Graiguenamanagh, County Kilkenny, is on the far bank. Take care if crossing as there is no footpath. The bridge was built in the 1760s, but was partly destroyed during the 1798 Rebellion. You can walk up the slim, twisting main street of Graigue to see Duiske Abbey, which was founded in 1204.

Arriving here, the waymarkers at Graigue seemed to suggest that the Barrow Way crosses the bridge, but it does not. Stay on the left bank towards St Mullin's. You pass Tinnahinch Castle, which dates from the 1540s and guarded the previous wooden bridge, and then the Upper Tinnahinch and Lower Tinnahinch Locks, and their respective weirs. The wooded valley steepens, and the river winds into a wall of trees. The soft high woods were tinted with pastel reds and yellows when I passed in early autumn.

Ballykeenan Lock

Past Carriglead Weir there is another short side canal to the lock, the oldest on the navigation, where there is a fine stone lock cottage. Further on you will see an ancient-looking piece of granite known as Freeney's Chair, supposedly for a highwayman who would sit here to watch the spot where his loot was buried on Brandon Hill, which rises to the west.

Bahana Wood is now to your left. Various sources suggest the wood gets its name from *beith*, the Irish for birch. The wood does have birch, but there are also stately oaks, ash, beech and sycamore, and bigger conifers like Douglas fir, Scots pine, Norwegian spruce and Japanese larch.

You come to the final weir on the Barrow navigation, and the side canal past it brings you to St Mullin's Lock. From here south, though you are still far inland, the Barrow becomes tidal. Past the lock the air turns brackish. The Barrow Way continues for another 1km to the Mullichain Cafe, which is sited in a renovated old grain store, and open seasonally. Here the Barrow Way ends.

Nearing the end of the Barrow Way

St Mullin's is a popular spot for twaite shad fishing early each summer. The twaite shad, a relative of herring and sprat, is anadromous, meaning it migrates from the sea to freshwater to spawn, coming up the Barrow to St Mullin's each May. St Mullin's has a rich ecclesiastical history. St Moling founded a monastery here in the seventh century, and legend says he spent seven years digging a stream to power his mill. By climbing the hill you can see the remains of a round tower, abbey and bell tower. There is also a granite high cross thought to date from the ninth century, and a former Church of Ireland church, now a museum and heritage centre. There is a Norman motte and bailey nearby too.

THE DERRY RIVER

Railway Walk & Tomnafinnoge Wood River Walk
(County Wicklow)

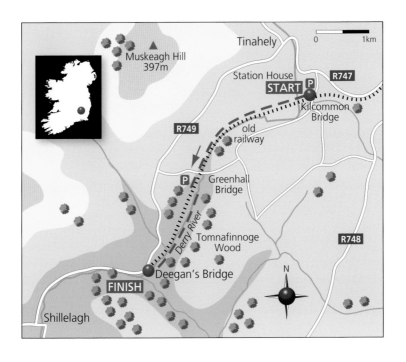

Tall oaks in Tomnafinnoge

Overview: Linear walk down a wooded lane through farmland and then into old oak woods.

Trail: From the Kilcommon Bridge car park to Tomnafinnoge, you are following the Railway Walk. Once in Tomnafinnoge, you are following the River Walk (blue arrows). You can also take a diversion on to the Oak Walk (green arrows).

Suitability: Fairly easy walk on wide paths.

Trailhead: Follow signs for the Railway Walk from the R747 on the east side of Tinahely. The car park and trailhead are just outside the town on the L3216. Bus Éireann has an infrequent service to Tinahely.

Distance & time: The Railway Walk from Kilcommon Bridge to Tomnafinnoge is almost 3km one way. The River Walk in Tomnafinnoge is a 4km return walk from the car park and back, or you can return by the Oak Walk which will add a few hundred metres. In total, walking the Railway Walk and River Walk from Kilcommon Bridge and back will be almost 10km. About 2½ to 3½ hours.

Alternative routes: You can also walk for 3.5km in the opposite direction to Tomnafinnoge from Kilcommon Bridge, by going left before the bridge rather than under it. There are lots of other marked trails near Tinahely; see www.tinahely.ie.

Map & further info: Railway Walk trail map available to download at www. irishtrails.ie and www.tinahely.ie. There is no trail map of Tomnafinnoge available online. The area is covered by OSi *Discovery Series* Sheet 62. A leaflet detailing local trails is available in Tinahely.

S outh of the Wicklow Mountains, the Derry River traverses one of Ireland's most iconic oak woods on its journey to the Slaney. From the trailhead, follow the track past the 'Railway Walk' stone, through young oaks. Take the path to the right under Kilcommon Bridge and out through pasture.

The Railway Walk

This trail follows the old railway line that once ran from Shillelagh to Tinahely, and on to meet the Rosslare–Dublin line at Woodenbridge. The Earl Fitzwilliam, owner of the Coolattin estate, donated land for the line and paid for its construction. There is an old station house near the trailhead. The line closed in 1945, going the way of all Ireland's rural railways, and the tracks were later removed. The local community reopened the route as a walking trail in 2007.

The trail crosses the Derry River, leaves it for a while and then rejoins it. It follows a woody lane with rich mature hedgerows. I counted off the trees and shrubs as I went: oak, sycamore, beech, elder, alder, willow, hawthorn, blackthorn, birch, holly and hazel.

When I walked here in early autumn, the river was a clear sepia, shallow enough for cattle to wade into it and drink. I found a fly agaric mushroom, a white-and-red toadstool right out of *Alice in Wonderland*, growing by the trail.

Built on an old rail line, surrounded by farms and forestry and bordered by rich hedgerows, this lane seems to exist right on the edge between the man-made and natural. This gives it more depth and texture than if it belonged completely to either world.

Through thick foliage I got only glimpses of the river, and in places fallen trees lay prostrate across it. I saw many downed trees on my rambles while researching this book, probably laid low by the vicious storms of early 2014. However, deadfall like this can benefit the ecology of a river, creating fresh pools and adding new complexity to the habitat.

After nearly 3km the lane brings you under Greenhall Bridge and into Tomnafinnoge Wood. Turn left for the car park and trailhead, and follow the blue markers for the River Walk onto a timber boardwalk through birches. The trail crosses the Derry River and then follows it on a gravel path. When I passed here, children were wading into the shallow brook with nets, seeking out fish and river bugs. The Derry has brown trout and the odd salmon, too.

The Derry River in Tomnafinnoge Wood

The Derry River in autumn

Tomnafinnoge is a fragment of the vast sessile oak woods of the Coolattin estate, owned by the Earls of Fitzwilliam. The wood is regarded as ancient, though like many of Ireland's oldest woods it was exploited over the centuries. Most of the oaks here were planted during the eighteenth century in existing woodland.

Timber from Coolattin, produced on deep rich soils, was used in the construction of King's College Chapel in Cambridge, Westminster Hall in London, the Old Library at Trinity College Dublin, and the Stadt House in Amsterdam, among other great buildings. This vast estate once covered almost one fifth of Wicklow. But during the great land clearances after the Famine, when higher rates were demanded from landowners for each tenant, the Fitzwilliams sent 6,000 people to Canada.

When the Coolattin estate was sold in the 1970s, it had over 500 wooded hectares. Almost one third of this was oak wood, most of which was felled during the 1970s and 1980s, but after much public protest the last 66-hectare fragment of oak wood at Tomnafinnoge was saved.

The Derry River was previously murky, silted up and prone to flooding. But when the National Parks and Wildlife Service took over management of the wood, it restored the river, which was a clear amber when I visited. This has also helped the oaks to regenerate naturally, by restoring drier conditions.

Follow the trail straight along the river, ignoring side paths. When I walked here in early autumn, the thickets of bracken and brambles, holly and hazel hid the river. The oaks seem to get taller and statelier as you go deeper into Tomnafinnoge. Coming from Galway, where our oceanic oak woods are scraggy and stunted, I found these trees to be a revelation. Their size commands your reverence and attention.

The great-spotted woodpecker, a bird rare in Ireland, has been breeding at Tomnafinnoge since 2009. Local birder Jimmy Murphy tells me there are sparrowhawks and buzzards in the wood too, as well as more typical river residents like kingfishers and dippers. Summer visitors include chiffchaff, willow warbler, blackcap, wood warbler and the odd cuckoo.

In spring and early summer, you can see flowering wood sorrel, bluebells and primroses here. But there are also invasive species like laurel and rhododendron. The trail leaves the river for a while, and further down there is a stone inscribed with lines written by the poet Jerome Stephens, who campaigned to save the

Great-spotted woodpecker in Tomnafinnoge Wood (courtesy Jimmy Murphy)

woods: 'The seed that bears my soul will fly and I shall live forever.' Stephens suffered from haemophilia and received a HIV-infected blood transfusion; he died in 1993.

The trail rejoins the river as it nears an old bridge, and passes some immense Scots pine. 'It looks prehistoric,' my companion said, staring up at one vast red trunk. The river draws close again as you near a barrier and then come to the bridge, a good place to linger and watch the water.

Turn back and follow the trail along the river. You can continue straight back to the Tomnafinnoge car park along the river, or turn off right on the green trail to see big oak stands deeper in the wood.

Ash, elder and willow over the Derry River

THE AVONMORE

River Walk, Avondale Forest Park
(County Wicklow)

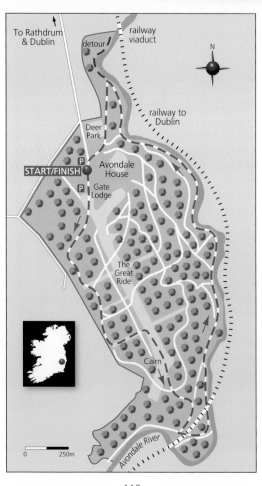

Overview: Looped walk on dramatic forest and riverside trails.

Trail: You are following the River Walk (white waymarkers with black footprints & arrows). There are plans to alter the trail network at Avondale in the coming years, so this route could change.

Suitability: The trail is graded moderate and mostly follows forest tracks. Some of the sections along the river are rough underfoot.

Trailhead: Avondale Forest Park is about 2.5km south of Rathdrum, County Wicklow, on the L2149. Rathdrum is serviced by Irish Rail on the Dublin–Rosslare line, and also by Bus Éireann from Dublin. There is a charge for parking.

Distance & time: 5km, 2 to 2½ hours.

Alternative routes: The River Walk is the longest of six trails at Avonmore, at the time of writing. Some of the shorter trails are multi-access (suitable for buggies and wheelchairs).

Services: Shops, pubs and accommodation in Rathdrum.

Map & further info: Trail map & info at www.coillteoutdoors.ie. The area is also covered by OSi *Discovery Series* Sheet 62.

Forest trails by the river

113

Avondale was the home and birthplace of Charles Stewart Parnell, the great campaigner for Irish Home Rule. But before anything else, Avondale is a place of trees. The estate was planted in 1770 by the forester Samuel Hayes, a barrister who also commissioned the architect James Wyatt to design Avondale House.

Hayes sought to foster an appreciation of trees in Ireland. He was a leading member of the Dublin Society when it encouraged the planting of 70 million trees, and he authored Ireland's first tree-planting manual. The oldest trees at Avondale – principally beeches, oaks, larches and silver firs – are from his time here. On his death, Hayes left Avondale to his cousin and fellow MP John Parnell, Charles Stewart's great grandfather. In 1904 the government bought the estate and began planting different tree species to study their growth. Avondale later became a forestry school.

Waking here from Rathdrum in June, I watched a peregrine falcon wheeling lazily in the sky above the forest.

From the car park, follow the white waymarkers for the River Walk down a lane left of the map board and then turn right. This road turns into a rougher track and passes under cedar, maple, beech, oak, fir, pine and larch. Soon the trail swings left into darker woods.

Keep with the River Trail waymarkers as you pass through a few junctions. Look out for a waymarker on a beech tree by a grassy lawn on your left. Turn left and follow the path between the grass and beeches. You can either continue along the lawn, or follow a side trail into the forest.

If you take the latter route, go left where the trail forks in two, near some Scots pine. I found puffball mushrooms growing in the woods here too. Soon you come to the Great Ride, the long, grass avenue that divides Avondale in two.

Head for the big cairn, which was apparently built by forestry students taking down old boundary walls on the estate. From here there are long

The long, grassy avenue at Avonmore, known as the Great Ride

views south towards the Vale of Avoca and Croaghan Kinsella. The Great Ride is lined with plots of different tree species, usually an acre in size. The lessons learned here have been applied widely to Irish silviculture.

Looking out on the Avonmore River

Cross to the other side of the Great Ride, and turn right along the edge of the forest. Follow the waymarker that directs you onto a narrow trail into the woods. When you reach the junction, take the second left by a bench to go downhill. Now you should start to hear the Avonmore River below. The waymarkers direct you down to the valley floor, where the trail goes left above the river.

Low water on the Avonmore (courtesy Elias Spinn)

There are still conifers here, but more natural woods too, with beech, oak, holly and hazel. The trail goes under the Dublin–Rosslare railway line twice, and passes remnants of Parnell's old sawmill. You will also get glimpses of the river below.

It might just be an illusion, caused by being at very floor of this valley, but the trees seem to get bigger now. There are huge redwoods, silver firs and sequoias. Redwoods are a favourite habitat of the treecreeper, which works its way up the trunk picking off insects. When it reaches the top, it flies down to the bottom and starts climbing again.

Carry on straight, ignoring any side trails, until you reach steps leading right. Take these down to the river. On the far bank, forested slopes drop to the riverbank. When I walked here, the Avonmore was flowing dark and quick, high on energy but lacking volume. In places, still black pools formed on the river, near shingle beaches.

The Avondale is not regarded as a great Irish river, but perhaps it should be. What it lacks in length and volume it makes up with spirit. Its name, after all, is *Abhainn Mór*, 'the big river', and everything down here feels vast, from the height of the spruces and firs to the breadth of the river. Even the ferns seem supersized.

Avondale has four trees on the Tree Council of Ireland's list of champion trees, including a noble fir with the second widest girth of any Irish tree, and a Douglas fir that is Ireland's second tallest tree. (Ireland's tallest tree is

Conifers grow tall in the shelter of the Avondale River valley

a Douglas fir on Wicklow's Powerscourt Estate. At 61.5m, it is just over half the height of the world's tallest tree, a coastal redwood in California).

The trail goes right at a fork; you then come to a great curve in the river, where it whitens as it flows over the rocky bed. The Avonmore holds eel and brown trout, and also introduced rainbow trout. Look too for a stream entering the river on the far bank through an old tunnel. Ignore any side trails leading left and keep with the river.

The trail crosses a footbridge over a pond. This was bulging with tadpoles when I passed in June. The path here is rough and knotted with tree roots, and you will still see oak, beech and ash amid the vertiginous conifers. I also found tutsan growing down here, a native shrub that produces toxic berries.

The trail climbs some steps, where signs advise you to 'mind your child' (I didn't have one with me). Then it crosses a stream and climbs back down to the river. Above you here is a spot known as Lover's Leap, though the origin of the name is unclear.

Eventually you come to a junction where the River Trail turns left and leaves the Avonmore. But you can also carry on along the river to a high railway viaduct, where the Avonmore bends and

Railway viaduct over the Avonmore, on the Dublin–Rosslare line

quickens. The woods down here feel more Irish than most of Avondale, with ash, willow, alder, rowan, hazel, hawthorn and oak. From the viaduct, turn around and walk back to the junction, then go right and leave the river. Climbing the valley wall, you can look out into a deep sea of towering trunks.

When you reach a junction, take the first narrow trail on your right, into dark woods. This will bring you to an eighteenth-century gate lodge for Avondale House, near the car park, and out of this tremendous forest.

THE AVONMORE

Blue Loop, Vale of Clara Nature Reserve
(County Wicklow)

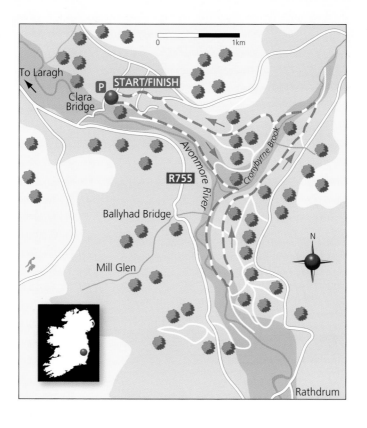

Walking through birches at Clara Vale

Overview: Looped walk up and down the slopes of the Avonmore River valley, through ancient woodland interspersed with conifers.

Trail: You are following the blue arrows for the duration of the walk.

Suitability: Moderate walk on forest tracks that are mostly easy underfoot, but there is a fair bit of ascending and descending.

Trailhead: Roughly halfway between Rathdrum and Laragh on the R755, turn onto the L6120, signposted for Clara Vale RC church. About 500m up this road on your right-hand side is the entrance to the Vale of Clara Nature Reserve, with space for a few cars. Rathdrum is serviced by Irish Rail and Bus Éireann. Laragh is serviced by St Kevin's Bus Service (www. glendaloughbus.com).

Distance & time: 9.5km, 2½ to 3½ hours.

Alternative routes: There are also shorter trails of 5.6km and 2km at Clara, and plenty of other unmarked tracks through the forest.

Services: Shop and pub at Rathdrum and Laragh.

Map & further info: OSi *Discovery Series* Sheet 56 covers most of Clara Vale. The map shows forest tracks but the blue trail is not specifically marked.

The author wading into the Avonmore (courtesy Una McMahon)

Sheltered by the Avonmore valley, the Vale of Clara guards one of Ireland's most extensive old oak woods. Clara shows you how Irish river valleys once looked.

From the entrance follow the track straight through two junctions, staying on the main path. The blue trail you are following will arrive back to the second junction from the left at the end of the walk. Most of the oaks are here in the northern part of the reserve, and there are also birch and hazel along the trail, which descends towards the river. This river flows from Lough Dan, above Roundwood, until it meets the Avonbeg below Rathdrum. Their confluence forms the Avoca.

In places here you can look around and see nothing but oak and birch, and down in this valley, both species grow tall. Clara feels like the primordial forest of Ireland; I half expected to hear wolves howling. 'There aren't many places in Ireland where you feel like you could get lost in the woods,' one of my companions said.

Stick with the blue arrows as the red and green walks veer off. The sun was hot when I walked here in mid-June, but the foliage offered shade and the sound of the river was cooling. You reach the riverside, but thick foliage means you cannot get to the water.

An oak dips gracefully over the Avonmore (courtesy Una McMahon)

However, where you meet the Cronybyrne Brook, you can take a rough path to your right down to the Avonmore. The water was clear and low, so I took off my socks and shoes and walked out into a knee-deep pool. In the middle of the river, I could see nothing but trees, water and rock. I scanned the water for jumping brown trout, but saw none.

Back on the main path, walk up along the stream and cross the footbridge. Just over the bridge look for an inscribed stone dedicated in 1999 to a ninety-year-old hillwalker, Jack Horsham. You then rejoin the Avonmore through more oak and birch. Naturalist Coilin MacLochlainn tells me dippers, kingfishers and goosander all frequent the river here.

Embankment above the Avonmore River

Near the riverside I watched a pink-and-red cinnabar moth float near blue and red damselflies. On hot summer days, the banded demoiselle damselfly – shining metallic green – is also abundant here.

Continue straight along the river until a junction where the blue arrow points left – turn here to leave the river and climb. You eventually go through a series of junctions as the trail meanders up through the woods – follow the blue arrow at each.

The native woods at Clara are interspersed with planted conifers, but the National Parks and Wildlife Service has removed species like Douglas fir, Norway spruce and western hemlock to let the woods regenerate. There are lots of young birch that, after the conifers were removed, colonised the acidic soils. Bird and bat boxes have also been installed, the latter to encourage pied flycatchers, a rare summer visitor.

Clara was the first place, in 2009, that a great-spotted woodpecker nest was found in the Republic of Ireland (one had been discovered in Northern Ireland three years earlier). It is thought this species was once native to Ireland, but in modern history it had been only an

Grove of tall oaks at Clara Vale

Conifers amid the broadleaf woods at Clara

occasional visitor. Clara is also home to long-eared owls, woodcocks and treecreepers.

High in the woods you get occasional glimpses west to Lugnaquilla, Leinster's highest mountain at 925m. From other clearings you can see nothing but wooded hills. At one point I looked into the understorey and saw oaks filling the space to the edge of my vision. I imagined the woods might go on like this forever, but then I would pass some exotic conifers, and the effect was lost. By one junction, we had a long staring contest with one fallow deer deep in the trees.

Clara was once part of the vast Watson-Wentworth estate, which covered 36,000 hectares. The estate coppiced its oak woods to provide timber for shipbuilding, construction and ironworks, cordwood for charcoal, and bark for tanning. But the demand for timber declined, and the woods regenerated. Many of the oaks here were planted during the nineteenth century, but some may be much older. 'Like all native woodlands, [Clara] was exploited down through the millennia but it is likely that some of this area has been continuously under woodland cover since forests emerged after the last Ice Age almost 13,000 years ago,' the forester Donal Magner writes in *Stopping By Woods: a Guide to the Forests and Woodlands of Ireland*.

You cross another footbridge over the Cronybyrne Brook, and the trail meanders through more junctions – again, just follow the blue arrows at each. You go down oak-lined avenues, and the waymarkers direct you out to a barrier. Follow the blue arrows left down the road. You pass some fields and houses. Keep your eyes out for a waymarker in the foliage on the left, and follow the trail back into the wood. You soon arrive back at the junction you passed near the start of the walk. Turn right here for the car park, to leave this fragment of ancient Ireland behind you.

THE VARTRY

Waterfall Walk, The Devil's Glen
(County Wicklow)

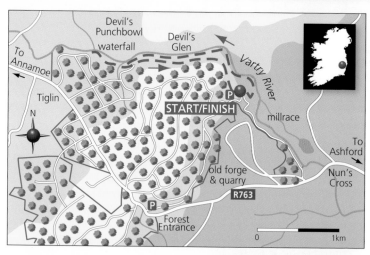

Looking across the wooded Vartry ravine (courtesy Una McMahon)

122

Overview: Dramatic looped walk on a forest trail that climbs up and down the slopes of a deep gorge.

Trail: You are following the Waterfall Walk (red arrows). The trail may, of course, be walked in the opposite direction too.

Suitability: Graded Moderate. Will not trouble fit walkers but there is quite an amount of ascending and descending, and the trails can be rough underfoot. Slippery conditions near the falls. Steep drops along the trail.

Trailhead: Devil's Glen car park. From Ashford, County Wicklow, take the R763 towards Annamoe/Laragh. The entrance to the Devil's Glen is on your right after 3.7km. Follow the forest road up to the car park. Ashford is serviced by Bus Éireann from Dublin.

Distance & time: 5km, 2 to 2½ hours.

Services: Shops, pubs and food in Ashford.

Map & further info: Trail maps available at www.coillteoutdoors.ie. The area is also covered by OSi *Discovery Series* Sheet 56.

*Walking under Douglas firs in the Devil's Glen
(courtesy Una McMahon)*

The deep, wooded valleys of Wicklow are inspiriting. The Vartry River rises under the Great Sugar Loaf and later flows through the Devil's Glen, a ravine near Ashford. Though you cannot see it, Glanmore Castle, the ancestral home of the Synge family, is on the hillside below. The playwright John Millington Synge visited the castle occasionally.

From the back of the car park at the trailhead, follow the red arrow onto a path by a stone wall. The sound of the river grows as you walk into the valley through Douglas firs. The trail goes left at a fork, then right, turning sharply down the valley walls.

Where the trail forks and a sign for the car park points

right, go left to keep heading down. The trail descends through hairpin bends. Keep an eye out for white arrows near the ground pointing the way. You reach a T-junction at the bottom. The waymarkers here were slightly confusing when I passed, but turn left to reach the river.

Here the Vartry is clogged with boulders once dropped by glaciers, forming a complicated series of pools and rapids. It was hot and close when I walked here in summer, and I slapped at flies as they landed on my neck. The water was running low, but on a humid day even the sight of a river is cooling.

The vegetation changes down here, becoming more natural than the plantations above. Ash and alder thrive in the damp, rich soils; ferns, mosses and liverworts spring from everywhere, and there is lots of holly, willow and hazel. In spring and early summer, before the canopy closes over, look for bluebells, wood anemone, primrose and wild garlic. The glen has more than eighty species of plants in total, including twenty-four trees.

The Devil's Punchbowl waterfall on the Vartry River (courtesy Una McMahon)

Follow the river for about 2km until the canopy opens and the river softens, and you can look out to conifer stands across the water. You pass a sharp turn left, but ignore it for now and continue straight. The woods close in again and the river's power grows.

Follow the steps up (take care: they may be slippery) to the waterfall, known as the Devil's Punchbowl. This whole valley is named after the falls, which was once said to roar so loudly that it sounded satanic, before the river was dammed upstream near Roundwood to create the Vartry Reservoir.

When I stopped here to rest, the sky greyed and rain began to fall. But the shower passed, and sunlight washed through the valley again. Mountaineers are fond of eulogising the light at high altitude but they should spend more time in deep, wooded valleys like this. When the sun comes out here light streams into the ravine at constantly changing angles, filtered on the way down by millions of leaves and branches. Then it hits the surface of the river, shattering.

Near the waterfall is a limestone plaque engraved with the words: 'When we find the ring, I'll propose.' This is part of the 'Stone Voices' collection by the artist Suky Best. It features personal stories of the Devil's Glen, pared down to a few words, engraved in stone near the site of each story. There are twenty-two plaques around the glen, with odd engravings such as: 'I see a small cart pulled by dogs' and 'We will hide here after the battle'.

Lush foliage along the Waterfall Walk (courtesy Una McMahon)

From the waterfall, walk back to the fork in the path and take the upper track to the right. The path climbs steadily and there are steep drops to your left. Ignore a side trail swinging back to the right by a bench, and continue straight. The trail crosses a couple of footbridges and goes through a rock arch.

High above the river you can see across to the other fact of this ravine, a primal mosaic of wood and rock. Sessile oak, downy birch, mountain ash and Scots pine cling to the steep faces, where ravens and peregrine falcons nest. Greywacke and shale – formed

Footbridge high above the Devil's Glen (courtesy Una McMahon)

from mud, sand and silt deposited in ancient seas – form the bedrock of the Devil's Glen.

Writing in *The Scenery and Antiquities of Ireland* in 1841, J. Stirling Coyne and N. P. Willis said of the Devil's Glen: 'We know no spot better for the indulgence of deep meditation …' They suggested it be named the Glen of the Gods instead.

It might feel like this gorge has been undisturbed for millennia, but the glen was replanted during the eighteenth century. During the 1798 Rebellion, Republican forces that had attacked the British at Newtownmountkennedy retreated here. The British set fire to the wood, smoking the rebels out, and massacred those who were found.

The Devil's Glen later became a popular tourist destination, and even had its own tea rooms. Artists such as James Arthur O'Connor

Walking through birch and rowan in the Devil's Glen (courtesy Una McMahon)

and George Barrett painted landscapes of the glen in late eighteenth and early nineteenth centuries.

Follow the trail until you reach a junction by timber sculptures. You will have seen other carvings along the walk. These are part of Coillte's Sculpture in Woodlands programme, though some of the works have been ravaged by the weather and removed.

Two Seamus Heaney lines are engraved on a bench here: 'The riverbed, dried-up, half-full of leaves. / Us, listening to a river in the trees.' Heaney had a home nearby, and some of his early poems were inspired by his time here, including the 'Glanmore Sonnets', in which the poet observed deer being 'careful under larch and May-green spruce'. The other trail at the Devil's Glen is named for him, and has benches along its route inscribed with his poetry.

From the junction, follow the red arrow to take a sharp turn right and climb upwards. Follow the path straight back to the car park.

Select Bibliography

Ireland is blessed with a rich local literature. This is a list of the most the most important sources from which I have drawn information. Some of the books listed here may be out of print, but are nonetheless worth tracking down.

Books

Delany, Ruth, *The Grand Canal of Ireland* (Lilliput Press, 1995; first published 1973 by David & Charles)

Delany, Ruth, *Guide to the Grand Canal of Ireland* (Dublin Stationery Office, 1995). Published online at www.iwai.ie.

Devlin, Zoë, *The Wildflowers of Ireland: A Field Guide* (The Collins Press, 2014).

Feehan, John, *The Landscape of Slieve Bloom: A Study of its Natural and Human Heritage* (Blackwater Press, 1979)

Fennell, Aubrey, *Heritage Trees of Ireland* (The Collins Press, 2013).

Fewer, Michael, *The Way-marked Trails of Ireland* (Gill & Macmillan, 1996)

Gordon, John D. & Wright, G. N., *A Topographical History of Great Britain and Ireland* (Chapman and Hall, 1833)

Guide to the Royal Canal of Ireland (4th edition, Waterways Ireland, 1997). Available online at www.iwai.ie.

Hanna, Peter & Co, *Guide to the Barrow Navigation* (Waterways Service & IWAI, 1998). Published online at www.iwai.ie.

Hannigan, Ken & Nolan, William (eds.), *Wicklow: History & Society* (Geography Publications, 1994)

Harbison, Peter, *Treasures of the Boyne Valley* (Gill & Macmillan, 2003)

Heaney, Paddy, *At the Foot of Slieve Bloom: History and Folklore of Cadamstown* (Kilcormac Historical Society, 2000)

Illingworth, Ruthin Mary Farrell (ed.) *Mullingar: Essays on the History of a Midlands Town in the 19th Century* (Westmeath County Library, 2002)

Joyce, Thomas P., *Bladhma: Walks of Discovery in Slieve Bloom* (Thomas P. Joyce, 1995)

Kavanagh, Art, *Ireland, 1798: The Battles* (Bunclody, County Wexford: Irish Family Names, 1998)

McCormack, Stephen and Regan, Eugenie, *Insects of Ireland: An Illustrated Introduction* (The Collins Press, 2014).

Magner, Donal, *Stopping by Woods: A Guide to the Forests and Woodlands of Ireland* (Lilliput Press, 2010)

Moriarty, Christopher, *Down the Dodder: Wildlife, History, Legend, Walks* (Wolfhound Press, 1991)

Mulhall, Mary & O'Flynn, Joan, *Treasures of Lucan* (Treasures of Lucan, 2007)

Nugent, Frank, *In Search of Peaks, Passes & Glaciers* (The Collins Press, 2013).

Ó Gibne, Claidhbh, *The Boyne Currach* (Four Courts Press, 2012)

Perrin, P. M. & Daly, O. H. 'A provisional inventory of ancient and long-established woodland in Ireland'. Irish Wildlife Manuals, No. 46. (National Parks and Wildlife Service, 2010)

Smith, Michael, *Shackleton: By Endurance We Conquer* (The Collins Press, 2014).

Whelan, Paul, *Lichens of Ireland: An illustrated introduction to over 250 species* (The Collins Press, 2013).

Wilde, William Robert, *The Beauties of the Boyne, and its Tributary*, the Blackwater (J. McGlashan, 1850)

Willis, N. P. & Coyne, J. S., *The Scenery and Antiquities of Ireland* (G. Virtue, 1842)

Wilson, Jim & Carmody, Mark, *The Birds of Ireland: A Field Guide* (The Collins Press, 2013).

Visitor's Guide: Devil's Glen Wood (Sculpture in Woodland, Coillte, December 2008)

Websites

The following websites have been good sources of information in researching these walks.

www.atheyeonthepast.blogpost.ie (Eye on the Past, a weekly historical column in the Kildare Nationalist, collected online here)

www.buildingsofireland.ie (National Inventory of Architectural Heritage)

www.coillteoutdoors.ie (Information on all recreation sites and trails managed by Coillte)

www.irishtrails.ie (Lists all national looped walks and long-distance trails in the Republic of Ireland)

www.iwai.ie (Inland Waterways Association of Ireland)

www.navanhistory.ie (Navan & District Historical Society)

www.offalyhistory.com (Offaly Historical & Archaeological Society)

www.royalcanal.net (Royal Canal Amenity Group)

www.slievebloom.ie (Details of walks in the Slieve Bloom area with information on local history and ecology)

www.waterwaysireland.org (Waterways Ireland).